Solitude

Part II

by

Johann Georg Zimmermann

Solitude
Part II
by Johann Georg Zimmermann

ISBN: 978-93-69073-00-9

Published by

DOUBLE 9 BOOKS

2/13-B, Ansari Road
Daryaganj, New Delhi – 110002
info@double9books.com
www.double9books.com
Tel. 011-40042856

ABOUT THE AUTHOR

Johann Georg Ritter von Zimmermann was a Swiss philosopher, naturalist, and physician, born on December 8, 1728, in Brugg, Switzerland. Zimmermann is known for his philosophical writings, particularly his exploration of solitude in the late 18th century. He served as the private physician to both George III of Britain and Frederick the Great of Prussia, an influential role that positioned him in the courts of Europe. Zimmermann's works blended naturalism, philosophy, and the human experience, offering insights into the nature of human emotions and intellectual growth. His writings, including Solitude, emphasized the importance of introspection and self-reflection for personal well-being and creativity. Throughout his life, Zimmermann engaged deeply with the intellectual currents of his time, contributing significantly to discussions on mental health and human nature. He died on October 7, 1795, in Hanover, Germany, at the age of 66. Zimmermann's legacy endures through his thought-provoking works that continue to be valued for their exploration of solitude, human nature, and the mind. He had one child, Katharina von Zimmermann, and remains an important figure in the history of European philosophy and medicine.

CONTENTS

PART II
The Pernicious Influence Of A
Total Seclusion From Society Upon
The Mind And The Heart

Chapter I
Introduction 7

Chapter II
Of the motives to solitude...15

Chapter III
The disadvantages of solitude...39

Chapter IV
The influence of solitude on the imagination....................53

Chapter V
The effects of solitude on a melancholy mind...................68

Chapter VI
The influence of solitude on the passions........................84

Chapter VII
Of the danger of idleness in solitude.............................116

Chapter VIII
Conclusion...121

PART II
THE PERNICIOUS INFLUENCE OF A TOTAL SECLUSION FROM SOCIETY UPON THE MIND AND THE HEART

Chapter I
Introduction

Solitude, in its strict and literal acceptation, is equally unfriendly to the happiness, and foreign to the nature of mankind. An inclination to exercise the faculty of speech, to interchange the sentiments of the mind, to indulge the affections of the heart, and to receive themselves, while they bestow on others, a kind assistance and support, drives men, by an ever active, and almost irresistible impulse, from solitude to society: and teaches them that the highest temporal felicity they are capable of enjoying, must be sought for in a suitable union of the sexes, and in a friendly intercourse with their fellow creatures. The profoundest deductions of reason, the highest flights of fancy, the finest sensibilities of the heart, the happiest discoveries of science, and the most valuable productions of art, are feebly felt, and imperfectly enjoyed, in the cold and cheerless regions of solitude. It is not to the senseless rock, or to the passing gale, that we can satisfactorily communicate our pleasures and our pains. The heavy sighs which incessantly transpire from the vacant bosoms of the solitary hermit and the surly misanthropist, indicate the absence of those high delights which ever accompany congenial sentiment and mutual affection. The soul sinks under a situation in which there are no kindred bosoms to participate its joys, and sympathise in its sorrows; and feels, strongly feels, that the beneficent Creator has so framed and moulded the temper of our minds, that society is the earliest impulse and the most powerful inclination of our hearts.

Society, however, although it is thus pointed out to us, as it were by the finger of the Almighty, as the means of reaching our highest possible state of earthly felicity, is so pregnant with dangers, that it depends entirely on ourselves, whether the indulgence of this instinctive propensity shall be productive of happiness or misery.

The pleasures of society, like pleasures of every other kind, must, to be pure and permanent, be temperate and discreet. While passion animates, and sensibility cherishes, reason must direct, and virtue be the object of our course. Those who search for happiness in a vague, desultory, and indiscriminate intercourse with the world; who imagine the palace of pleasure to be surrounded by the gay, unthinking, and volatile part of the species; who conceive that the rays of all human delight beam from places of public festivity and resort;

> "Who all their joys in mean profusion waste,
>
> Without reflection, management, or taste;
>
> Careless of all that virtue gives to please;
>
> For thought too active, and too mad for ease;
>
> Who give each appetite too loose a rein,
>
> Push all enjoyment to the verge of pain;
>
> Impetuous follow where the passions call,
>
> And live in rapture or not live at all;"

will, instead of lasting and satisfactory fruition, meet only with sorrowful disappointment. This mode of seeking society is not a rational indulgence of that natural passion which heaven, in its benevolence to man, has planted in the human heart; but merely a factitious desire, an habitual pruriency, produced by restless leisure, and encouraged by vanity and dissipation. Social happiness, true and essential social happiness, resides only in the bosom of love and in the arms of friendship, and can only be really enjoyed by congenial hearts and kindred minds, in the domestic bowers of privacy and retirement. Affectionate intercourse produces an inexhaustible fund of delight. It is the perennial sunshine of the mind. With what extreme anxiety do we all endeavor to find an amiable being with whom we may form a tender tie and close attachment, who may inspire us with unfading bliss, and receive increase of happiness from our endearments and attention! How greatly do such connexions increase the kind and benevolent dispositions of the heart! and how greatly do such dispositions, while they lead the mind to the enjoyment of domestic happiness, awaken all the virtues, and call forth the best and strongest energies of the soul! Deprived of the chaste and endearing sympathies of love and friendship, the species sink into gross sensuality or mute indifference, neglect the improvement of their faculties, and renounce all anxiety to please; but incited by these propensities, the sexes mutually exert their powers, cultivate their talents, call every intellectual energy into action; and, by endeavoring to promote each other's happiness, mutually secure their own.

Adverse circumstances, however, frequently prevent well disposed characters, not only from making the election which their hearts would prompt, and their understandings approve, but force them into alliances which both reason and sensibility reject. It is from the disappointments of love or of ambition that the sexes are generally repelled from society to solitude. The affection, the tenderness, the sensibility of the heart, are but too often torn and outraged by the cruelty and malevolence of an unfeeling world, in which vice bears on its audacious front the mask of virtue, and betrays innocence into the snares of unsuspected guilt. The victims, however, whether of love or of ambition, who retire from society to recruit their depressed spirits, and repair their disordered minds, cannot, without injustice, be stigmatized as misanthropists, or arraigned as anti-social characters. All relish for scenes of social happiness may be lost by an extreme and over ardent passion for the enjoyments of them; but it is only those who seek retirement from an aversion to the company of their fellow creatures, that can be said to have renounced, or be destitute of, the common sympathies of nature.

The present age, however, is not likely to produce many such unnatural characters, for the manners of the whole world, and particularly of Europe, were never, perhaps, more disposed to company. The rage for public entertainments seems to have infected all the classes of society. The pleasures of private life seem to be held in universal detestation and contempt; opprobrious epithets, defame the humble enjoyments of domestic love, and those whose hours are not consumed in unmeaning visits, or unsocial parties, are regarded as censors of the common conduct of the world, or as enemies to their fellow creatures; but although mankind appear so extremely social, they certainly were never less friendly and affectionate. Neither rank, nor sex, nor age, is free from this pernicious habit. Infants, before they can well lisp the rudiments of speech, are initiated into the idle ceremonies and parade of company: and can scarcely meet their parents or their playmates without being obliged to perform a punctilious salutation. Formal card parties, and petty treats, engross the time that should be devoted to healthful exercise and manly recreation. The manners of the metropolis are imitated with inferior splendor, but with greater absurdity, in the country; every village has its routs and its assemblies, in which the curled darlings of the place blaze forth in feathered lustre and awkward magnificence; and while the charming simplicity of one sex is destroyed by affectation, the honest virtues of the other by dissolute gallantry, and the passions of both inflamed by vicious and indecent mirth, the grave elders of the districts are trying their tempers and impoverishing their purses at sixpenny whist and cassino.

The spirit of dissipation has reached even the vagrant tribe. The Gypsies of Germany suspend their predatory excursions, and on one previously-appointed evening in every week, assemble to enjoy their guilty spoils in the fumes of strong waters and tobacco. The place of rendezvous is generally the vicinity of a mill, the proprietor of which, by affording to these wandering tribes an undisturbed asylum, not only secures his property from their depredations, but, by the idle tales with which they contrive to amuse his ear, respecting the characters and conduct of his neighbors, furnishes himself with new subjects of conversation for his next evening coterie.

Minds that derive all their pleasure from the levity and mirth of promiscuous company, are seldom able to contribute, in any high degree, to their own amusement. Characters like these search every place for entertainment, except their own bosoms and the bosoms of their surrounding families, where by proper cultivation, real happiness, the happiness arising from love and friendship, is alone capable of being found.

The wearied pleasurist, sinking under the weight that preys upon his spirits, flies to scenes of public gayety or private splendor, in fond but vain expectation that they will dispel his discontent, and recreate his mind; but he finds, alas! that the fancied asylum affords him no rest. The ever-craving appetite for pastime grows by what it feeds on; and the worm, which devoured his delight amidst his sylvan scenery of solitude, still accompanies him to crowded halls of elegance and festivity. While he eagerly embraces every object that promises to supply the dreadful vacancy of his mind, he exhausts his remaining strength; enlarges the wound he is so anxiously endeavoring to heal; and by too eagerly grasping at the phantom pleasure, loses, perhaps for ever, the substantial power of being happy.

Men whose minds are capable of higher enjoyments always feel these perturbed sensations, when deluded into a fashionable party, they find nothing to excite curiosity, or interest their feelings! and where they are pestered by the frivolous importunities of those for whom they cannot entertain either friendship or esteem. How, indeed, is it possible for a sensible mind to feel the slightest approbation, when a coxcomb enamored of his own eloquence, and swoln with the pride of self-conceited merit, tires by his loquacious nonsense, all around him?

The great Leibnitz was observed by his servant frequently to take notes while he sat at church; and the domestic very rationally conceived that he was making observations on the subject of the sermon: but it is more consistent with the character of this philosopher to conclude, that he was indulging the powers of his own capacious and excursive mind, when those of the preacher ceased to interest him. Thus it happens, that while the multitude are driven from solitude to society, by being tired of themselves, there are some, and those not a few, who seek refuge in rational retirement from the frivolous dissipation of company.

An indolent mind is as irksome to itself as it is intolerable to others; but an active mind feels inexhaustible resources in its own power. The first is forced to fly from itself for enjoyment, while the other calmly resigns itself to its own suggestions, and always meets with the happiness it has vainly sought for in its communion with the world.

To rouse the soul from that lethargy into which its powers are so apt to drop from the tediousness of life, it is necessary to apply a stimulus both to the head and to the heart. Something must be contrived to strike the senses and interest the mind. But it is much more difficult to convey pleasure to others, than to receive it ourselves; and while the many wait in anxious hope of being entertained, they find but few who are capable of entertaining. Disappointment increases the eagerness of desire; and the uneasy multitude rush to places of public resort, endeavoring, by noise and bustle, festive gratification, elegant decoration, rich dresses, splendid illuminations, sportive dances, and sprightly music, to awaken the dormant faculties, and agitate the stagnant sensibilities of the soul. These scenes may be considered the machineries of pleasure; they produce a temporary effect, without requiring much effort or co-operation to obtain it; while those higher delights, of which retirement is capable, cannot be truly enjoyed without a certain degree of intellectual exertion. There are, indeed, many minds so totally corrupted by the unceasing pursuits of these vain and empty pleasures, that they are utterly incapable of relishing intellectual delight; which, as it affords an enjoyment totally unconnected with, and independent of, common society, requires a disposition and capacity which common company can never bestow. Retirement, therefore, and its attendant enjoyments, are of a nature too refined for the gross and vulgar capacities of the multitude, who are more disposed to gratify their intellectual indolence, by receiving a species of entertainment which does not require from them the exertion of thought, than to enjoy pleasures of a nobler kind, which can only be procured by a rational restraint of the passions, and a proper exercise of the powers of the mind. Violent and tumultuous impressions can alone gratify such characters, whose pleasures like those of the slothful Sybarites, only indicate the pain they undergo in striving to be happy.

Men, eager for the enjoyment of worldly pleasures, seldom attain the object they pursue. Dissatisfied with the enjoyments of the moment, they long for absent delight, which seems to promise a more poignant gratification. Their joys are like those of Tantalus, always in view, but never within reach. The activity of such characters lead to no beneficial end; they are perpetually in motion, without making any progress: they spur on "the lazy foot of time," and then complain of the rapidity of its flight, only because they have made no good use of its presence: they "take no note of time but by its loss;" and year follows year, only to increase their uneasiness. If the bright beam of Aurora wake them from their perturbed repose, it is only to create new anxiety how they are to drag through the passing day. The change of season produces no change in their wearied dispositions; and every hour comes and goes with equal indifference and discontent.

The pleasures of society, however, although they are attended with such unhappy effects, and pernicious consequences, to men of weak heads and corrupted hearts, who only follow them for the purpose of indulging the follies, and gratifying the vices, to which they have given birth, are yet capable of affording to the wise and the virtuous, a high, rational, sublime, and satisfactory enjoyment. The world is the only theatre upon which great and noble actions can be performed, or the heights of moral and intellectual excellence usefully attained. The society of the wise and good, exclusive of the pleasing relaxation it affords from the anxieties of business, and the cares of life, conveys valuable information to the mind, and virtuous feelings to the breast. There experience imparts its wisdom in a manner equally engaging and impressive; the faculties are improved, and knowledge increased. Youth and age reciprocally contribute to the happiness of each other. Such a society, while it adds firmness to the character, gives fashion to the manners; and opens immediately to the view the delightful models of wisdom and integrity. It is only in such society that man can rationally hope to exercise, with any prospect of success, the latent principle, which continually prompts him to pursue the high felicity of which he feels his nature capable, and of which the Creator has permitted him to form a faint idea.

> "In every human heart there lies reclined
> Some atom pregnant with ethereal mind;
> Some plastic power, some intellectual ray,
> Some genial sunbeam from the source of day;
> Something that warms, and restless to aspire,
> Wakes the young heart, and sets the soul on fire;
> And bids us all our inborn powers employ
> To catch the phantom of ideal joy."

Sorrow frequently drives its unhappy victims from solitude into the vortex of society as a means of relief; for solitude is terrible to those whose minds are torn with anguish for the loss of some dear friend, whom death has, perhaps, taken untimely from their arms; and who would willingly renounce all worldly joys to hear one accent of that beloved voice, which used, in calm retirement, to fill his ear with harmony, and his heart with rapture.

Solitude also is terrible to those whose felicity is founded on popular applause; who have acquired a degree of fame by intrigue, and actions of counterfeited virtue; and who suffer the most excruciating anxiety to preserve their spurious fame. Conscious of the fraudulent means by which they acquire possession of it, and of the weak foundation on which it is built, it appears continually to totter, and always ready to overwhelm them in its ruins. Their attention is sedulously called to every quarter; and, in order to prop up the unsubstantial fabric, they bend with mean submission to the pride of power; flatter the vanity, and accommodate themselves to the vices of the great; censure the genius that provokes their jealousy; ridicule the virtue that shames the conduct of their patrons; submit to all the follies of the age; take advantage of its errors; cherish its prejudices; applaud its superstition, and defend its vices. The fashionable circles may, perhaps, welcome such characters as their best supporters and highest ornaments; but to them the calm and tranquil pleasures of retirement are dreary and disgusting.

To all those, indeed, whom vice has betrayed into guilt, and whose bosoms are stung by the adders of remorse, solitude is doubly terrible; and they fly from its shades to scenes of worldly pleasure, in the hope of being able to silence the keen reproaches of violated conscience in the tumults of society. Vain attempt!

Solitude, indeed, as well as religion, has been represented in such dismal, disagreeable colors, by those who were incapable of tasting its sweets, and enjoying its advantages, that many dismiss it totally from all their schemes of happiness, and fly to it only to alleviate the bitterness of some momentary passion, or temporary adversity, or to hide the blushes of approaching shame. But there are advantages to be derived from solitude, even under such circumstances, by those who are otherwise incapable of enjoying them. Those who know the most delightful comforts, and satisfactory enjoyments, of which a well regulated solitude is productive, like those who are acquainted with the solid benefits to be derived from religion, will seek retirement, in the hours of prosperity and content, as the only means by which they can be enjoyed in true perfection. The tranquillity of its shades will give richness to their joys; its uninterrupted quietude will enable them to expatiate on the fullness of their felicity; and they will turn their eyes with soft compassion on the miseries of the world, when compared with the blessings they enjoy.

Strongly, therefore, as the social principle operates in our breast; and necessary as it is, when properly regulated, to the improvement of our minds, the refinement of our manners, and the melioration of our hearts; yet some portion of our time ought to be devoted to rational retirement: and we must not conclude that those who occasionally abstain from the tumultuous pleasures, and promiscuous enjoyments of the world, are morose characters, or of peevish dispositions; nor stigmatize those who appear to prefer the calm delights of solitude to the tumultuous pleasures of the world, as unnatural and anti-social.

> "Whoever thinks, must see that man was made
>
> To face the storm, not languish in the shade:
>
> Action's his sphere, and for that sphere design'd,
>
> Eternal pleasures open on his mind.
>
> For this fair hope leads on th' impassion'd soul
>
> Through life's wild lab'rinths to her distant goal,
>
> Paints in each dream, to fan the genial flame,
>
> The pomp of riches, and the pride of fame;
>
> Or fondly gives reflection's cooler eye
>
> In solitude, an image of a future sky."

Chapter II
Of the motives to solitude

The motives which induce men to exchange the tumultuous joys of society, for the calm and temperate pleasures of solitude, are various and accidental; but whatever may be the final cause of such an exchange, it is generally founded on an inclination to escape from some present or impending constraint; to shake off the shackles of the world; to taste the sweets of soft repose; to enjoy the free and undisturbed exertion of the intellectual faculties; or to perform, beyond the reach of ridicule, the important duties of religion. But the busy pursuits of worldly minded men prevent the greater part of the species from feeling these motives, and, of course, from tasting the sweets of unmolested existence. Their pleasures are pursued in paths which lead to very different goals: and the real, constant, and unaffected lover of retirement is a character so rarely found, that it seems to prove the truth of lord Verulam's observation, that he who is really attached to solitude, must be either more or less than man; and certain it is, that while the wise and virtuous discover in retirement an uncommon and transcending brightness of character, the vicious and the ignorant are buried under its weight, and sink even beneath their ordinary level. Retirement gives additional firmness to the principles of those who seek it from a noble love of independence, but loosens the feeble consistency of those who only seek it from novelty and caprice.

To render solitude serviceable, the powers of the mind, and the sensibilities of the heart, must be co-equal, and reciprocally regulate each other; weakness of intellect, when joined with quick feelings, hurries its possessor into all the tumult of worldly pleasure; and when mingled with torpid insensibility, impels him to the cloister. Extremes, both in solitude and in society, are equally baneful.

A strong sense of shame, the keen compunctions of conscience, a deep regret for past follies, the mortification arising from disappointed hopes, and the dejection which accompanies disordered health, sometimes so affect the spirits, and destroy the energies of the mind, that the soul shrinks back upon itself at the very approach of company, and withdraws to the shades of solitude, only to brood and languish in obscurity. The inclination to retire, in cases of this description, arises from a fear of meeting the reproaches or disregard of an unpitying and unreflecting world, and not from that erect spirit which disposes the mind to self enjoyment.

The disgust arising from satiety of worldly pleasures, frequently induces a temporary desire for solitude. The dark and gloomy nature, indeed, of this disposition, is such as neither the splendors of a throne, nor the light of philosophy, are able to irradiate and dispel. The austere and petulant Heraclitus abandoned all the pleasures and comforts of society, in the vain hope of being able to gratify his discontented mind, by indulging an antipathy against his fellow creatures; flying from their presence he retired, like his predecessor Timon, to a high mountain, where he lived for many years among the beasts of the desert, on the rude produce of the earth, regardless of all the comforts a civilized society is capable of bestowing. Such a temper of mind proceeds from a sickened intellect and disordered sensibility, and indicates the loss of that fine, but firm sense of pleasure, from which alone all real enjoyment must spring. He who having tasted all that can delight the senses, warm the heart, and satisfy the mind, secretly sighs over the vanity of his enjoyments, and beholds all the cheering objects of life with indifference, is, indeed, a melancholy example of the sad effects which result from an intemperate pursuit of worldly pleasures. Such a man may, perhaps, abandon society, for it is no longer capable of affording him delight; but he will be debarred from all rational solitude, because he is incapable of enjoying it, and a refuge to the brute creation seems his only resource. I have, indeed, observed even noblemen and princes in the midst of abundance, and surrounded by all the splendor that successful ambition, high state, vast riches, and varying pleasures can confer, sinking the sad victims of satiety; disgusted with their glories; and dissatisfied with all those enjoyments which are supposed to give a higher relish to the soul; but they had happily enriched their minds with notions far superior to all those which flow from the corrupted scenes of vitiated pleasures; and they found, in solitude, a soft and tranquil pillow, which invited their perturbed minds, and at length lulled their feelings into calm repose. These characters were betrayed for a time by the circumstances which surrounded their exalted stations into an excess of enjoyment; but they were able to relish the simple occupations, and to enjoy the tranquil amusements of retirement, with as much satisfaction as they had formerly pursued the political intrigues of the cabinet, the hostile glories of the field, or the softer indulgences of peaceful luxury; and were thereby rendered capable of deriving comfort and consolation from that source which seems only to heighten and exasperate the miseries of those whose minds are totally absorbed in the dissipations of life.

The motives, indeed, which lead men either to temporary retirement, or absolute solitude, are innumerably various. Minds delicately susceptible to the impressions of virtue, frequently avoid society, only to avoid the pain they feel in observing the vices and follies of the world. Minds active and vigorous, frequently retire to avoid the clogs and incumbrances by which the tumults and engagements of society distract and impede the free and full enjoyment of their faculties. The basis, indeed, of every inclination to solitude is the love of liberty, either mental or corporeal; a freedom from all constraint and interruption: but the form in which the inclination displays itself, varies according to the character and circumstances of the individual.

Men who are engaged in pursuits foreign to the natural inclination of their minds, sigh continually for retirement, as the only means of recruiting their fatigued spirits, and procuring a comfortable repose. Scenes of tranquillity can alone afford them any idea of enjoyment. A refined sense of duty, indeed, frequently induces noble minds to sacrifice all personal pleasures to the great interests of the public, or the private benefits of their fellow creatures; and they resist every opposing obstacle with courage, and bear every adversity with fortitude, under those cheering sentiments, and proud delights, which result from the pursuits of active charity and benevolence, even though their career be thwarted by those whose advantages they design to promote. The exhilarating idea of being instrumental in affording relief to suffering humanity, reconciles every difficulty, however great: prompts to new exertions, however fruitless; and sustains them in those arduous conflicts, in which all who aspire to promote the interest, and improve the happiness of mankind, must occasionally engage, especially when opposed by the pride and profligacy of the rich and great, and the obstinacy and caprice of the ignorant and unfeeling. But the most virtuous and steady minds cannot always bear up against "a sea of troubles, or by opposing, end them:" and, depressed by temporary adversities, will arraign the cruelty of their condition, and sigh for the shades of peace and tranquillity. How transcendent must be the enjoyment of a great and good minister who, after having anxiously attended to the important business of the state, and disengaged himself from the necessary but irksome occupation of official detail, refreshes his mind in the calm of some delightful retreat, with works of taste, and thoughts of fancy and imagination! A change, indeed, both of scene and sentiment, is absolutely necessary, not only in the serious and important employments, but even in the common occupations and idle amusements of life. Pleasure springs from contrast. The most charming object loses a portion of its power to delight, by being continually beheld. Alternate society and solitude are necessary to the full enjoyment of both the pleasures of the world and the delights of retirement. It is, however, asserted that the celebrated Pascal, whose life was far from being inactive, that quietude is a beam of the original purity of our nature, and that the height of human happiness is in solitude and tranquillity. Tranquillity, indeed, is the wish of all: the good, while pursuing the track of virtue; the great while following the star of glory; and the little, while creeping in the styes of dissipation, sigh for tranquillity and make it the great object which they ultimately hope to attain. How anxiously does the sailor, on the high and giddy mast, when rolling through tempestuous seas, cast his eyes over the foaming billows, and anticipate the calm security he hopes to enjoy when he reaches the wished for shore! Even kings grow weary of their splendid slavery, and nobles sicken under increasing dignities. All, in short, feel less delight in the actual enjoyment of worldly pursuits, however great and honorable they may be, than in the idea of their being able to relinquish them and retire to

"… some calm sequestered spot;

The world forgetting, by the world forgot."

The restless and ambitious Pyrrhus hoped that ease and tranquillity would be the ultimate reward of his enterprising conquests. Frederic the great, discovered, perhaps unintentionally, how pleasing and satisfactory the idea of tranquillity was to his mind, when immediately after he had gained a glorious and important victory, he exclaimed on the field of battle, "Oh that my anxieties may now be ended!" The emperor Joseph also displayed the predominancy of his passion for tranquillity and retirement, when on asking the famous German pedestrian, Baron Grothaus, what countries he next intended to traverse, was told a long number in rapid succession. "And what then?" continued the emperor. "Why then," replied the baron, "I intend to retire to the place of my nativity, and enjoy myself in rural quietude, and the cultivation of my patrimonial farm." "Ah, my good friend," exclaimed the emperor, "if you will trust the voice of sad experience, you had better neglect the walk, and retire before it is too late, to the quietude and tranquillity you propose."

Publius Scipio, surnamed Africanus, during the time that he was invested with the highest offices of Rome, and immediately engaged in the most important concerns of the empire, withdrew whenever an opportunity occurred, from public observation, to peaceful privacy; and though not devoted, like Tully, to the elegant occupations of literature and philosophy, declared that "he was never less alone than when alone." He was, says Plutarch, incomparably the first both in virtue and power, of the Romans of his time; but in his highest tide of fortune, he voluntarily abandoned the scene of his glory, and calmly retired to his beautiful villa in the midst of a romantic forest, near Liturnum, where he closed, in philosophic tranquillity, the last years of a long and splendid life.

Cicero, in the plenitude of his power, at a time when his influence over the minds of his fellow citizens was at its height, retired, with the retiring liberties of his country, to his Tusculum villa, to deplore the approaching fate of his beloved city, and to ease, in soothing solitude, the anguish of his heart.

Horace, also, the gay and elegant favorite of the great Augustus, even in the meridian rays of royal favor, renounced the smiles of greatness, and all the seductive blandishments of an imperial court, to enjoy his happy muse among the romantic wilds of his sequestered villa of Tibur, near the lake Albunea.

But there are few characters who have passed the concluding scenes of life with more real dignity than the emperor Dioclesian. In the twenty-first year of his reign, though he had never practised the lessons of philosophy either in the attainment or the use of supreme power, and although his reign had flowed with a tide of uninterrupted success, he executed his memorable resolution of abdicating the empire, and gave the world the first example of a resignation which has not been very frequently imitated by succeeding monarchs. Dioclesian was at this period only fifty-nine years of age, and in the full possession of his mental faculties; but he had vanquished all his enemies, and executed all his designs; and his active life, his wars, his journeys, the cares of royalty, and his application to business having impaired his constitution, and brought on the infirmities of a premature old age, he resolved to pass the remainder of his days in honorable repose; to place his glory beyond the reach of fortune, and to relinquish the theatre of the world to his younger and more active associates. The ceremony of his abdication was performed in a spacious plain, about three miles from Nicomedia. The emperor ascended a lofty throne, and, in a speech full of reason and dignity, declared his intention both to the people and to the soldiers, who were assembled on this extraordinary occasion. As soon as he had divested himself of the purple, he withdrew from the gazing multitude; and traversing the city in a covered chariot, proceeded without delay to the favorite retirement which he had chosen in his native country of Dalmatia. The emperor, who, from a servile origin, had raised himself to the throne, passed the last nine years of his life in a private condition at Salona. Reason had dictated, and content seems to have accompanied, his retreat, in which he enjoyed for a long time the respect of those princes to whom he had resigned the possession of the world. It is seldom that minds long exercised in business have formed any habits of conversing with themselves, and in the loss of power, they principally regret the want of occupation. The amusements of letters and of devotion, which afford so many resources in solitude, were incapable of fixing the attention of Dioclesian: but he had preserved, or, at least, he soon recovered, a taste for the most innocent as well as natural pleasures; and his leisure hours were sufficiently employed in building, planting, and gardening. His answer to Maximian is deservedly celebrated. He was solicited by that restless old man to resume the reins of government and the imperial purple. He rejected the temptation with a smile of pity, calmly observing, that if he could show Maximian the cabbages he had planted at Salona, he should be no longer urged to relinquish the enjoyment of happiness for the pursuit of power. In his conversations with his friends he frequently acknowledged, that of all the arts the most difficult was that of reigning; and he expressed himself on that favorite topic with a degree of warmth which could be the result only of experience. "How often," was he accustomed to say, "is it the interest of four or five ministers to combine together to deceive the sovereign! Secluded from mankind by his exalted dignity, the truth is concealed from his knowledge: he can only see with their eyes; he hears nothing but their misrepresentations. He confers the most important offices upon vice and weakness, and disgraces the most virtuous and deserving among his subjects; and by such infamous acts the best and wisest princes are sold to the venal corruption of their courtiers." A just estimate of greatness, and the assurance of immortal fame, improve our relish for the pleasures of retirement.

Zenobia, the celebrated queen of Palmyra and the east; a female whose superior genius broke through the servile indolence imposed on her sex by the climate and manners of Asia, the most lovely as well as the most heroic of her sex, who spread the terror of her arms over Arabia, Armenia, and Persia, and kept even the legions of the Roman empire in awe, was, after the two great battles of Antioch and Emesa, at length subdued, and made the illustrious captive of the emperor Aurelian; but the conqueror, respecting the sex, the beauty, the courage and endowments of the Syrian queen, not only preserved her life, but presented her with an elegant villa at Tibur or Tivoli, about twenty miles from Rome; where, in happy tranquillity, she fed the greatness of her soul with the noble images of Homer, and the exalted precepts of Plato; supported the adversity of her fortunes with fortitude and resignation; and learnt that the anxieties attendant on ambition are happily exchanged for the enjoyments of ease and the comforts of philosophy.

Charles V. resigned the government of the empire to his brother the king of the Romans; and transferred all claims of obedience and allegiance to him from the Germanic body, in order that he might no longer be detained from that retreat for which he long had languished. In passing, some years before, from Valladolid to Placentia, in the Province of Estremadura, he was struck with the delightful situation of the monastery of St. Justus, belonging to the order of St. Jerome, not many miles distant from the town; and observed to some of his attendants, that this was a spot to which Dioclesian might have retired with pleasure. The impression remained upon his mind, and he determined to make it the place of his own retreat. It was seated in a vale of no great extent, watered by a small brook, and surrounded by rising grounds covered with lofty trees; and from the nature of the soil, as well as the temperature of the climate, was esteemed the most healthful and delicious situation in Spain. Some months before his resignation, he had sent an architect thither to add a new apartment to the monastery for his accommodation; but he gave strict orders that the style of the building should be such as suited his present station rather than his former dignity. It consisted only of six rooms; four of them in the form of friar's cells, with naked walls; the other two, each twenty feet square, were hung with brown cloth, and furnished in the most simple manner; they were all on a level with the ground, with a door on one side into a garden of which Charles himself had given the plan, and had filled it with various plants, which he intended to cultivate with his own hands. On the other side they communicated with the chapel of the monastery, in which he was to perform his devotions. In this humble retreat, hardly sufficient for the comfortable accommodation of a private gentleman, did Charles enter with twelve domestics only, and buried in solitude and silence his grandeur, his ambition, and all those vast projects which, during almost half a century, had alarmed and agitated Europe; filling every kingdom in it by turns with the terror of his arms, and the dread of being subdued by his power.

These instances of resignation and retirement, to which many others might have been added, sufficiently prove that a desire to live in free leisure, independent of the restraints of society, is one of the most powerful affections of the human mind; and that solitude, judiciously and rationally employed, amply compensates all that is sacrificed for the purpose of enjoying it.

But there are many other resources from whence an anti-social disposition may arise, which merits consideration. That terrible malady, the hypocondria, frequently renders the unhappy sufferer not only averse to society in general, but even fearful of meeting a human being; and the still more dreadful malady a wounded heart, increases our antipathy to mankind. The fear of unfounded calumny also sometimes drives weak and dejected minds into the imaginary shelter of obscurity; and even strong and honest characters, prone to disclose their real sentiments, are disgusted at the world from a consciousness of its being unable to listen temperately to the voice of truth. The obstinacy with which mankind persist in habitual errors, and the violence with which they indulge inveterate passions, a deep regret for their follies, and the horror which their vices create, drives us frequently from their presence. The love of science, a fondness for the arts, and an attachment to the immortal works of genius, induce, I trust, not a few to neglect all anxiety to learn the common news of the day, and keep them in some calm, sequestered retreat far from the unmeaning manners of the noisy world, improving the genuine feelings of their hearts, and storing their minds with the principles of true philosophy. There are others, though I fear they are few, who, impressed by a strong sense of the duties of religion, and feeling how incompatible with their practice are most, if not all, the factitious joys of social life, retire from the corrupted scene, to contemplate, in sacred privacy, the attributes of a Being unalterably pure, and infinitely good; to impress upon their minds so strong a sense of the importance of obedience to the divine will, of the value of the reward promised to virtue, and the terrors of the punishment denounced against crimes, as may overbear all temptations which temporal hope or fear can bring in their way, and enable them to bid equal defiance to joy and sorrow; to turn away at one time from the allurements of ambition, and press forward at another against the threats of calamity.

The dejection occasioned by the hypochondria renders the mind not only averse from, but wholly incapable of, any pleasure, and induces the unhappy sufferer to seek a solitude by which it is increased. The influence of this dreadful malady is so powerful, that it destroys all hope of remedy, and prevents those exertions, by which alone, we are told it can be cured.

> To cure the mind's wrong bias—spleen,
>
> Some recommend the bowling-green;
>
> Some, hilly walks; all, exercise;
>
> Fling but a stone, the giant dies;
>
> Laugh, and be well. Monkies have been
>
> Extreme good doctors for the spleen;
>
> And kittens, if the humor hit,
>
> Have harlequined away the fit.

But, alas! the heart shuts itself against every pleasing sensation, and the mind dismisses every cheering sentiment. Joy opens in vain its festal arms to receive him; and he shuns embraces, whose light and mirthful air would only serve to increase the melancholy of his dreary and distempered mind. Even the tender, affectionate offices of friendship, in endeavoring to sooth and divert his mind by lively conversation and social intercourse, appear officious and ill-timed. His spirits are quite dejected; his faculties become torpid; and his sense of enjoyment is annihilated. The charming air which breathes to us the sweetest fragrance, and most invigorating delights, feels to him like a pestilent congregation of vapors.

> His pensive spirit takes the lonely grove
>
> Nightly he visits all the sylvan scenes,
>
> Where, far remote, a melancholy moon
>
> Raising her head, serene and shorn of beams,
>
> Throws here and there the glimmerings through the trees,
>
> To make more awful darkness.

Conscious that his frame is totally unstrung, and that his pulse is incapable of beating in any pleasant unison with the feelings of his healthful friends, he withers into sorrowful decay. Every object around him appears to be at enmity with his feelings, and comes shapeless and discolored to his disordered eyes. The gentle voice of pity grates his ears with harsh and hollow sounds, and seems to reproach him with insulting tones. Stricken by his dreadful malady, the lamentable effects of which a cruel and unfeeling world so often ridicule and despise, and constantly tearing open the wound it has occasioned, the afflicted spirit flies from every scene of social joy and animating pleasure, seeks as a sole resource, to hide its sorrows in solitary seclusion, and awaits, in lingering sufferance, the stroke of death.

The erroneous opinions, perverse dispositions, and inveterate prejudices of the world, are sometimes the causes which induce men to retire from society, and seek in solitude the enjoyments of innocence and truth. Careless of a commerce with those for whom they can entertain no esteem, their minds naturally incline toward those scenes in which their fancy paints the fairest form of felicity. He, indeed, whose free and independent spirit is resolved to permit his mind to think for itself; who disdains to form his feelings, and to fashion his opinions, upon the capricious notions of the world; who is too candid to expect that others should be guided by his notions, and sufficiently firm not to obey implicitly the hasty notions of others; who seeks to cultivate the just and manly feelings of the heart, and to pursue truth in the paths of science, must detach himself from the degenerate crowd, and seek his enjoyments in retirement. For to those who love to consult their own ideas, to form opinions upon their own reasonings and discernment, and to express only such sentiments as they really feel, a society whose judgments are borrowed, whose literature is only specious, and whose principles are unfounded, must not only be irksomely insipid, but morally dangerous. The firm and noble minded disdain to bow their necks to the slavish yoke of vulgar prejudice, and appeal, in support of their opinions, to the higher tribunal of sense and reason, from the partial and ill-formed sentences of conceited critics, who, destitute themselves of any sterling merit, endeavor to depreciate the value of that coin whose weight and purity render it current, and to substitute their own base and varnished compositions in its stead. Those self-created who proudly place themselves in the professor's chair, look with an envious and malignant eye on all the works of genius, taste, and sense; and as their interests are intimately blended with the destruction of every sublime and elegant production, their cries are raised against them the moment they appear. To blast the fame of merit is their chief object and their highest joy: and their lives are industriously employed to stifle the discoveries, to impede the advancement, to condemn the excellency, and to pervert the meaning of their more ingenious contemporaries. Like loathsome toads, they grovel on the ground, and, as they move along, emit a nasty slime, or frothy venom, on the sweetest shrubs and fairest flowers of the fields.

From the society of such characters, who seem to consider the noble productions of superior intellect, the fine and vigorous flights of fancy, the brilliant effusions of a sublime imagination, and the refined feelings of the heart, as fancied conceits or wild deliriums, those who examine them by a better standard than that of fashion or common taste, fly with delight.

The reign of envy, however, although it is perpetual as to the existence of the passion, is only transitory as to the objects of its tyranny; and the merit which has fallen the victim of its rage, is frequently raised by the hand of truth, and placed on the throne of public applause. A production of genius, however the ears of its author were deafened, during his life, by the clamors of calumny, and hisses of ignorance, is reviewed with impartiality when he dies, and revived by the acclamations of ingenuous applause. The reproach which the life of a great and good man is continually casting on his mean and degenerate contemporaries, is silenced by his death. He is remembered only in the character of his works; and his fame increases with the successive generations, which his sentiments and opinions contribute to enlighten and adorn.

The history of the celebrated English philosopher, David Hume, affords, perhaps, a stronger instance of the dangers to which wit and learning are exposed from the malicious shafts of envy, ignorance, and intolerance, than that of any other author. The tax indeed, is common to authors of every description, but it frequently falls the heaviest on the highest heads. This profound philosopher and elegant historian, possessed a mild temper; a lively, social disposition; a high sense of friendship, and incorruptible integrity. His manners, indeed, appeared, at first sight, cold and repulsive; for he had sacrificed little to the graces: but his mind was invariably cheerful, and his affections uncommonly warm and generous: and neither his ardent desire of fame, nor the gross and unfounded calumnies of his enemies, were capable of disturbing the happy tranquillity of his heart. His life was passed in the constant exercise of humanity and benevolence; and even those who had been seduced, by the jealous and vindictive artifices of others, wantonly to attack his fame and character with obloquy and reproach, experienced his kindness, and acknowledged his virtues. He would never indeed confess that his friends had ever had occasion to vindicate any one circumstance of his character or conduct, or that he had ever been attacked either by the baleful tooth of envy, or the rage of civil or religious faction. His company, indeed, was equally agreeable to all classes of society; and young and old, rich and poor, listened with pleasure to his conversation, and quitted his company with regret; for although he was deeply learned, and his discourses replete with sagacity and science, he had the happy art of delivering his sentiments upon all subjects without the appearance of ostentation, or in any way offending the feelings of his hearers.

The interests of religion are said to have suffered by the abuse of his talents; but the precepts of Christianity were never more powerfully recommended, than by the integrity of his morals, and the purity of his life. His benign and gentle spirit, attached to virtue, and averse from every species of vice, essentially promoted the practice of piety, and the duties of a religious mind; and did not, as is always the case with the zeal of persecution and martyrdom, tear away the very foundation of that fabric which it pretends to support. The excellency, indeed, both of the head and the heart of this great and good man, enabled him not only to enjoy himself with perfect felicity, but to contribute to the improvement, and increase the happiness of mankind. This is the opinion now generally entertained of the character of Hume; but far different were the sentiments of his contemporaries upon this subject. It was neither in a barbarous country, or in an unenlightened age, that he lived; but although the land was free, the people philosophical, and the spirit of the times provoked the minds of learned men to metaphysical inquiry, the fame of Hume was wrecked upon his moral and religious writings. He was charged with being a sceptic; but from the propagation of certain doctrines, and the freedom of inquiry which had then gone forth, it is impossible to attribute his disappointments to this cause. A kind of natural prejudice, indeed, prevailed in England at this period against the Scots; but as he did not experience much favor from his own countrymen, no conclusion can be fairly drawn from this circumstance; and the extraordinary History of his Literary Transactions, a work written by himself, cannot be perused without an equal degree of surprise and concern. The contemptuous repulses which his several compositions received from the public, appear incredible; but the facts he relates are undoubtedly authentic; and while they raise a sorrowful regret for the fate of Hume in particular, they most unhappily tend to diminish the ardor of the student, who contemplates the various dangers to which his desire of fame may be exposed, and may, perhaps, induce him to quit the pursuit of an object "so hard to gain, so easy to be lost."

The melancholy history of the literary career of the celebrated Hume, as appears from the short sketch he made of *his own life*, while he calmly waited, under an incurable disorder, the moment of approaching dissolution; a work which proclaims the mildness, the modesty, and the resignation of his temper, as clearly as his other works demonstrate the power and extent of his mind. The history, indeed, of every man who attempts to destroy the reigning prejudices, or correct the prevailing errors, of his age and country, is nearly the same. He who has the happiness to see objects of any description with greater perspicuity than his contemporaries, and presumes to disseminate his superior knowledge, by the unreserved publication of his opinions, sets himself up as a common mark for the shafts of envy and resentment to pierce, and seldom escapes from being charged with wicked designs against the interests of mankind. A writer, whatever his character, station, or talents may be, will find that he has a host of malevolent inferiors ready to seize every opportunity of gratifying their humbled pride, by attempting to level his superior merits, and subdue his rising fame. Even the compassionate few, who are ever ready to furnish food to the hungry, clothing to the naked, and consolation to the afflicted, seldom feel any other sensation than that of jealousy on beholding the wreath of merit placed on the brow of a deserving rival. The Ephesians, with republican pride, being unable to endure the reproach which they felt from the pre-eminency of any individual, banished to some other state, the citizen who presumed to excel the generality of his countrymen. It would be, in some measure, adopting this egregious and tyrannical folly, were I to exhort the man whose merits transcend those who are his equals in rank, or station, to break off all intercourse and connexion with them; but I am certain that he might, by an occasional retirement, elude the effects of their envy, and avoid those provocations to which, by his superiority, he will otherwise be continually exposed.

To treat the frailties of our fellow creatures with tenderness, to correct their errors with kindness, to view even their vices with pity, and to induce, by every friendly attention, a mutual complacency and good will, is not only an important moral duty, but a means of increasing the sum of earthly happiness. It is, indeed, difficult to prevent an honest mind from bursting forth with generous indignation against those artful hypocrites who, by specious and plausible practices, obtain the false character of being wise and good, and obtrude their flimsy and heterodox opinions upon the unthinking world, as the fair and genuine sentiments of truth and virtue. The anger which arises in a generous and ardent mind, on hearing a noble action calumniated, or a useful work illiberally attacked, is not easily restrained; but such feelings should be checked and regulated with a greater degree of caution than even if they were less virtuous and praiseworthy; for, if they are indulged with frequency, their natural violence may weaken the common charities of the mind, and convert its very goodness and love of virtue into a mournful misanthropy, or virulent detestation of mankind.

Let not the man, whose exalted mind, improved by study and observation, surveys with a discriminating eye the moral depravities and mental weaknesses of human nature, submit to treat his envious inferiors with inveterate anger, and undistinguishing revenge. Their envy as a tribute of approbation to his greatness. Let him look with the gentle eye of pity upon those who err rather from the wicked suggestions of others, than from the malevolence of their own hearts: let him not confound the weak and innocent reptile with the scorpion and the viper; let him listen, without emotion, to the malignant barking and envious hissings that everywhere attend the footsteps of transcendent merit; let him disregard, with philosophic dignity, the senseless clamors of those noisy adversaries who are blinded by prejudice, and deaf to the arguments of sense and reason: let him rather, by a mild and forbearing temper, endeavor to make some impression on their hearts; and if he should find their bosoms susceptible, he may hope in time to convince them of their errors, and, without violence or compulsion, bring back their deluded understandings to a sense of truth, and the practice of virtue; but, if experience convince him that every endeavor to reform them is fruitless and vain, let him—

> Neglect the grumblers of an envious age,
>
> Vapid in spleen, or brisk in frothy rage;
>
> Critics, who, ere they understand, defame;
>
> And seeming friends who only do not blame,
>
> And puppet prattlers, whose unconscious throat
>
> Transmits what the pert witling prompts by rote:
>
> Let him neglect this blind and babbling crowd,
>
> To enjoy the favor of the wise and good.

Slander, however, by fixing her talons on the most virtuous characters, generally defeats her own malice, and proclaims their merit. It may, indeed, tend to diminish their inclination for general society, and to render them, in some degree, apprehensive of the danger of even well deserved fame. "Durable fame," says Petrarch, "is only to be derived from the practice of virtue, and from such works as are worthy of descending from generation to generation. As to praters, gowned gentlemen, that walk in their silks, glitter in their jewels, and are pointed at by the people, all their bravery and pomp, their show of knowledge, and their thundering speeches, last only with their lungs, and then vanish into thin smoke; for the acquisition of wealth, and the desires of ambition, are no witnesses of true desert. I think I shall have fame after my death; and that is a fame from which no profit is derived; but, on the contrary, frequently injures, while alive, the person who is to enjoy it when dead. What procured the destruction of Cicero, Demosthenes, and Zeno, but foul and haggard envy of their fame? What brought the chosen men of the great ship Argos to Colchis, but the fame of that king's riches? For what else was signified by the Golden Fleece, but the riches seized by these marauders, destitute of true riches, and who were clad with fleeces not their own?" Many, indeed, whose merits have cast a radiance around their characters, have hidden its splendors with the shades of retirement to avoid giving uneasiness to envy; and, by being deprived of that warm and aspiring tribute of applause which they had gloriously and justly earned, have, in some instances at least, indulged too keen a sense of the depravity of mankind. Solon, after having in vain exhorted the Athenians to resist the tyranny of Pisistratus, and save the liberties of that country, on which he had conferred such distinguished services, returned to his own house, and placing his weapons at the street door, exclaimed, as a last effort, "*I have done all in my power to save my country and defend its laws!*" and then retired from the tumults of public life, to weep in silence over the servility of the Athenians, and the fate of Athens. History affords many illustrious instances, both ancient and modern, of the like kind: for there never was a statesman, who possessed a great mind and manly feelings, that did not, even during the plentitude of his power, occasionally wish to escape from the incorrigible vices which prevail in courts, to the enjoyment of the more innocent pleasures and humble virtues which surround the cottage. Such exalted characters cannot observe, without the highest disgust, and keenest indignation, the virtues of the best, and the services of the bravest men of the nation, blasted by the envious breath of brainless placemen, or the insidious insinuations of female favorites, whose whole time is employed in caressing their monkies and paroquets, or in aspersing the merits of those who boldly seek their fortune by the open and manly road of true desert, and not by the deep, dark, and crooked paths of flattery and intrigue. Can such a man behold the double dealing and deceitful artifices by which the excellency of princes is corrupted, their imaginations dazzled, their discernment blinded, and their minds led astray without feeling uncommon indignation? Certainly not. But however acutely his bosom may feel, or tongue express his sense of such prevailing practices, he must still be forced to see, with even a more contemptuous and painful sensation, that envious rage and jealous asperity, which burst from the cringing crowd of mean and abject courtiers, on hearing the monarch, in the grateful feelings of his heart, applaud the eminent and faithful services of some gallant officer. Dion was the principal statesman at the court of Dionysius, and the deliverer of Sicily. When the younger Dionysius succeeded to the throne of his father, Dion, in the first council that he held, spoke with so much propriety on the existing state of affairs, and on the measures which ought to be taken, that the surrounding courtiers appeared to be mere children in comparison. By the freedom of his counsels he exposed, in a strong light, the slavish principles of those who, through a timorous disingenuity, advised such measures as they thought would please their prince, rather than such as might advance his interest. But what alarmed them most, were the steps he proposed to take with regard to the impending war with Carthage; for he offered either to go in person to Carthage, and settle an honorable peace with the Carthagenians, or, if war should be inevitable, to fit out and maintain fifty gallies at his own expense. Dionysius was pleased with the magnificence of his spirit; but his courtiers felt that it made them appear little; and agreeing that, at all events, Dion was to be crushed, they spared for that purpose no calumny that malice could suggest. They represented to the king that this favorite certainly meant to make himself master by sea, and by that means to obtain the kingdom for his sister's children. There was, moreover, another and obvious cause of their hatred to him, in the reserve of his manners, and the sobriety of his life. They led the young and ill-educated king through every species of debauchery, and were the shameless panders of his wrong directed passions. Their enmity to Dion, who had no taste for luxurious enjoyments, was a thing of course; and as he refused to partake with them in their vices, they resolved to strip him of his virtues; to which they gave the name of such vices as are supposed to resemble them. His gravity of manners they called pride; his freedom of speech, insolence; his declining to join in their licentiousness, contempt. It is true, there was a natural haughtiness in his deportment and an asperity that was unsociable, and difficult of access; so that it was not to be wondered at if he found no ready admission to the ears of a young king, already spoiled by flattery. Willing to impute the irregularities of Dionysius to ignorance and bad education, Dion endeavored to engage him in a course of liberal studies, and to give him a taste for those sciences which have a tendency to moral improvement. But in this wise and virtuous resolution he was opposed by all the artifices of court intrigue.

Men, in proportion as their minds are dignified with noble sentiments, and their hearts susceptible of refined sensibility, feel a justifiable aversion to the society of such characters, and shrink from the scenes they frequent; but they should cautiously guard against the intrusions of that austerity and moroseness with which such a conduct is but too apt to inspire the most benevolent minds. Disgusted by the vices and follies of the age, the mind becomes insensibly impressed with a hatred toward the species, and loses, by degrees, that mild and humane temper which is so indispensably necessary to the enjoyment of social happiness. Even he who merely observes the weak or vicious frailties of his fellow creatures with an intention to study philosophically the nature and disposition of man, cannot avoid remembering their defects with severity, and viewing the character he contemplates with contempt, especially if he happens to be the object of their artifices, and the dupe of their villanies. Contempt is closely allied with hatred; and hatred of mankind will corrupt, in time, the fairest mind: it tinges, by degrees, every object with the bile of misanthropy; perverts the judgment; and at length looks indiscriminately with an evil eye on the good and bad, engenders suspicion, fear, jealousy, revenge, and all the black catalogue of unworthy and malignant passions: and when these dreadful enemies have extirpated every generous sentiment from the breast, the unhappy victim abhors society, disclaims his species, sighs, like St. Hyacinth, for some distant and secluded island, and with savage barbarity, defends the inviolability of its boundaries by the cruel repulsion, and, perhaps, the death of those unhappy mortals whom misfortune may drive, hapless and unpitied, to its inhospitable shores.

But if misanthropy be capable of producing such direful effects on well disposed minds, how shocking must be the character whose disposition, naturally rancorous, is heightened and inflamed by an habitual hatred and malignancy toward his fellow creatures! In Swisserland, I once beheld a monster of this description; I was compelled to visit him by the duties of my profession; but I shudder while I recollect the enormity of his character. His body was almost as deformed as his mind. Enmity was seated on his distorted brow. Scales of livid incrustation, the joint produce of his corrupted body and distempered mind, covered his face. His horrid figure made me fancy that I saw Medusa's serpents wreathing their baleful folds among the black and matted locks of his dishevelled hair; while his red and fiery eyes glared like malignant meteors through the obscurity of his impending eyebrows. Mischief was his sole delight, his greatest luxury, and his highest joy. To sow discord among his neighbors, and to tear open the closing wounds of misery, was his only occupation. His residence was the resort of the disorderly, the receptacle of the vicious, and the asylum of the guilty.

Collecting around him the turbulent and discontented of every description, he became the patron of injustice, the protector of villany, the perpetrator of malice, the inventer of fraud, the propagator of calumny, and the zealous champion of cruelty and revenge; directing, with malignant aim, the barbed shafts of his adherents equally against the comforts of private peace and the blessings of public tranquillity. The bent and inclination of his nature had been so aggravated and confirmed by the "multiplying villanies of his life," that it was impossible for him to refrain one moment from the practice of them, without feeling uneasiness and discontent; and he never appeared perfectly happy, but when new opportunities occurred to glut his infernal soul with the spectacle of human miseries.

The Timon of Lucian was in some measure excusable for his excessive hatred to mankind, by the unparallelled wrongs they had heaped upon him. The inexorable antipathy he entertained against the species had been provoked by injuries almost too great for the common fortitude of humanity to endure. His probity humanity, and charity to the poor, had been the ruin of him; or rather his own folly, easiness of disposition, and want of judgment in his choice of friends. He never discovered that he was giving away his all to wolves and ravens. Whilst these vultures were preying on his liver, he thought them his best friends, and that they fed upon him out of pure love and affection. After they had gnawed him all round, ate his bones bare, and whilst there was any marrow in them, sucked it carefully out, they left him cut down to the roots and withered; and so far from relieving him, or assisting him in their turns, would not so much as know or look upon him. This made him turn a common laborer; and, dressed in his skin garment, he tilled the earth for hire; ashamed to show himself in the city, and venting his rage against the ingratitude of those who, enriched, as they had been by him now proudly passed along without noticing him. But although such a character is not to be despised or neglected, no provocation, however great can justify the violent and excessive invectives which he profanely bellowed forth from the bottom of Hymettus; "this spot of earth shall be my only habitation while I live; and when I am dead, my sepulchre. From this time forth, it is my fixed resolution to have no commerce or connexion with mankind; but to despise them, and avoid it. I will pay no regard to acquaintance, friendship, pity or compassion. To pity the distressed, or to relieve the indigent, I shall consider as a weakness, nay, as a crime; my life, like that of the beasts of the field, shall be spent in solitude; and Timon alone shall be Timon's friend. I will treat all beside as enemies and betrayers. To converse with them were profanation! to herd with them impiety. Accursed be the day that brings them to my sight! I will look upon men, in short, as no more than so many statues of brass or stone; will make no truce, have no connexion with them. My retreat shall be the boundary to separate us for ever. Relations, friends, and country, are empty names, respected by fools alone. Let Timon only be rich and despise all the world beside. Abhorring idle praise, and odious flattery, he shall be delighted with himself alone. Alone shall he sacrifice to the gods, feast alone, be his own neighbor, and his own companion. I am determined to be alone for life; and when I die, to place the crown upon my own head. The fairest name I would be distinguished by is that of a misanthrope. I would be known and marked out by my asperity of manners; by moroseness, cruelty, anger, and inhumanity. Were I to see a man perishing in the flames, and imploring me to extinguish them, I would throw pitch or oil into the fire to increase it; or, if the winter flood should overwhelm another, who, with out-stretched hands should beg me to assist him, I would plunge him still deeper in the stream, that he might never rise again. Thus shall I be revenged of mankind. This is Timon's law, and this hath Timon ratified. I should be glad, however, that all might know how I abound in riches, because that I know will make them miserable."

The moral to be drawn from this dialogue of the celebrated Grecian philosopher, is the extreme danger to which the best and most benevolent characters may be exposed, by an indiscreet and unchecked indulgence of those painful feelings with which the baseness and ingratitude of the world are apt to wound the heart. There are, however, those who, without having received ill treatment from the world, foster in their bosoms a splenetic animosity against society, and secretly exult in the miseries and misfortunes of their fellow creatures. Indulging themselves in the indolent habits of vice and vanity, and feeling a mortification in being disappointed of those rewards which virtuous industry can alone bestow, they seek a gloomy solitude to hide them from those lights which equally discover the errors of vice and the rectitude of virtue. Unable to attain glory for themselves, and incapable of enduring the lustre of it in others, they creep into discontented retirement, from which they only emerge to envy the satisfaction which accompanies real merit, to calumniate the character to which it belongs; and, like satan, on the view of paradise, to "see undelighted all delight."

There are, however, a class of a very different description, who, unoppressed by moody melancholy, untinctured by petulance or spleen, free from resentment, and replete with every generous thought and manly sentiment, calmly and contentedly retire from society, to enjoy, uninterruptedly, a happy communion with those high and enlightened minds, who have adorned by their actions the page of history, enlarged by their talents the powers of the human mind, and increased by their virtues the happiness of mankind.

Retirement, however solitary it may be, when entered into with such a temper of mind, instead of creating or encouraging any hatred toward the species, raises our ideas of the possible dignity of human nature; disposes our hearts to feel, and our hands to relieve, the misfortunes and necessities of our fellow creatures; calls to our minds what high capacious powers lie folded up in man; and giving to every part of creation its finest forms, and richest colors, exhibits to our admiration its brightest glories and highest perfections, and induces us to transplant the charm which exists in our own bosoms into the bosoms of others.

> ... The spacious west,
>
> And all the teeming regions of the south,
>
> Hold not a quarry, to the curious flight
>
> Of knowledge, half so tempting, or so fair,
>
> As man to man: nor only where the smiles
>
> Of love invite; nor only where the applause
>
> Of cordial honor turns the attentive eye
>
> On virtue's graceful deeds; for since the course
>
> Of things external acts in different ways
>
> On human apprehension, as the hand
>
> Of nature tempered to a different frame
>
> Peculiar minds, so haply where the powers
>
> Of fancy neither lessen nor enlarge
>
> The images of things, but paint, in all
>
> Their genuine hues, the features which they wear
>
> In nature, there opinions will be true,
>
> And action right....

A rational solitude, while it corrects the passions, improves the benevolent dispositions of the heart, increases the energies of the mind, and draws forth its latent powers. The Athenian orator, Callistratus, was to plead in the cause which the city of Oropus had depending; and the expectation of the public was greatly raised, both by the powers of the orator, which were then in the highest repute, and the importance of the trial. Demosthenes, hearing the governors and tutors agree among themselves to attend the trial, with much importunity prevailed on his master to take him to hear the pleaders. The master having some acquaintance with the officer who opened the court, got his young pupil a seat where he could hear the orators without being seen. Callistratus had great success, and his abilities were extremely admired. Demosthenes was fired with the spirit of emulation. When he saw with what distinction the orator was conducted home, and complimented by the people, he was struck still more with the power of that commanding eloquence which would carry all before it. From this time, therefore, he bade adieu to the other studies and exercises in which boys are engaged, and applied himself with great assiduity to declaiming, in hope of being one day numbered among the orators. Satyrus, the player who was an acquaintance of his, and to whom he lamented, after having been for some time called to the bar, "that though he had almost sacrificed his health to his studies, he could gain no favor with the people," promised to provide him with a remedy, if he would repeat some speech in Euripides or Sophocles. When Demosthenes had finished his recitation, Satyrus pronounced the same speech; and he did it with such propriety of action, and so much in character, that it appeared to the orator quite a different passage; and Demosthenes now understanding how much grace and dignity of action adds to the best oration, quitted the practice of composition, and, building a subterraneous study repaired thither, for two or three months together, to form his action, and exercise his voice; and, by this means formed that strong, impassioned, and irresistible eloquence, which rendered him the glory of Athens, and the admiration of the world. Most of the exalted heroes, both of Greece and Rome, who devoted their attention to arts and to arms, acquired their chief excellency in their respective pursuits, by retiring from public observation, and cultivating their talents in the silence of solitude. St. Jerome, the most learned of all the Latin fathers, and son of the celebrated Eusebius, retired from the persecution of religious fury into an obscure and dreary desert in Syria, where he attained that rich, animated, and sublime style of eloquence, which afterward so essentially contributed to support the rising church, and to enlighten while it dazzled the Christian world. The Druids, or ministers of religion among the ancient Gauls, Britons, and Germans, retired, in the intervals of their sacred functions, into awful forests and consecrated groves, where they passed their time in useful study and pious prayers; and while they acquired a complete knowledge of astrology, geometry, natural philosophy, politics, geography, morals, and religion, rendered themselves happy and revered, and produced, by the wise instruction they were capable of affording to others, but particularly to youth, whose education they superintended, a bright succession of priests, legislators, counsellors, judges, physicians, philosophers, and tutors, to the respective nations in which they resided.

The modern Julian, the justly celebrated Frederic, king of Prussia, derives the highest advantages from his disguised retirement at Sans Souci, where he contrives the means of hurling inevitable destruction against the enemies of his country; listens to and relieves with all the anxiety of a tender parent, the complaints and injuries of his meanest subjects; and recreates his excursive mind, by revising and correcting his immortal works for the admiration of posterity. Philosophy, poetry, and politics, are the successive objects of his attention; and while he extends his views, and strengthens his understanding, by the study of ancient wisdom, he meliorates his heart by the delightful offerings of the muses, and increases the public strength by the wise and economical management of his resources. An awful silence, interrupted only by gentle airs with which it is refreshed, pervades this delightful retreat. It was during the twilight of an autumnal evening that I visited this solemn scene. As I approached the apartment of this philosophic hero, I discovered him sitting, "nobly pensive," near a small table, from which shone the feeble rays of a common taper. No jealous sentinels, or ceremonious chamberlain, impeded my progress by scrutinizing inquiries of suspicion and mistrust; and I walked free and unchecked, except by respect and veneration, through the humble unostentatious retreat of this extraordinary man. All characters, however high and illustrious they may be, who wish to attain a comprehensive view of things, and to shine in the highest spheres of virtue, must learn the rudiments of glory under the discipline of occasional retirement.

Solitude is frequently sought from an inclination to extend the knowledge of our talents and characters to those with whom we have no opportunity of being immediately acquainted; by preparing with greater care, and closer application, for the inspection of our contemporaries, works worthy of the fame we are so anxious to acquire: but it seldom happens, alas! that those whose labors are most pregnant with instruction and delight, have received, from the age or country in which they lived, or even from the companions with whom they associated, the tribute of kindness or applause that is justly due to their merits. The work which is stigmatized and traduced by the envy, ignorance, or local prejudices of a country, for whose delight and instruction it was particularly intended, frequently receives from the generous suffrages of impartial and unprejudiced strangers, the highest tribute of applause. Even those pretended friends, under whose auspices it was at first undertaken, upon whose advice it proceeded, and upon whose judgment it was at length published, no sooner hear its praises resounded from distant quarters, than they permit the poisoned shafts of calumny to fly unaverted around the unsuspecting author, and warrant, by their silence, or assist, by their sneers, every insidious insinuation against his motives or his principles. This species of malevolence has been feelingly painted by the celebrated Petrarch. "No sooner had my fame," says he, "risen above the level of that which my contemporaries had acquired, than every tongue babbled, and every pen was brandished against me: those who had before appeared to be my dearest friends, instantly became my deadliest enemies: the shafts of envy were industriously directed against me from every quarter: the critics, to whom my poetry had before been much more familiar than their psalms or their prayers, seized, with malignant delight, every opportunity of traducing my morals; and those with whom I had been most intimate, were the most eager to injure my character, and destroy my fame." The student, however, ought not to be discouraged by this instance of envy and ingratitude. He who, conscious of his merit, learns to depend only on himself for support, will forget the injustice of the world, and draw his comfort and satisfaction from more infallible sources: like the truly benevolent and great, he will confer his favors on the public without the expectation of a return; and look with perfect indifference upon all the efforts his treacherous friends, or open enemies, are capable of using. He will, like Petrarch, appeal to posterity for his reward; and the justice and generosity of future ages will preserve his fame to succeeding generations, heightened and adorned in proportion as it has been contemporaneously mutilated and depressed.

The genius of many noble minded authors, particularly in Germany, are obscured and blighted by the thick and baneful fogs with which ignorance and envy overwhelm their works. Unable to withstand the incessant opposition they meet with, the powers of the mind grow feeble and relaxed; and many a fair design and virtuous pursuit is quitted in despair. How frequently does the desponding mind exclaim, "I feel my powers influenced by the affections of the heart. I am certainly incapable of doing to any individual an intentional injury, and I seek with anxiety every opportunity of doing good; but, alas! my motives are perverted, my designs misrepresented, my endeavors counteracted, my very person ridiculed, and my character defamed." There are, indeed, those whose courage and fortitude no opposition can damp, and no adversity subdue; whose firm and steady minds proceed with determined resolution to accomplish their designs in defiance of all resistance; and whose bright talents drive away the clouds of surrounding dulness, like fogs before the sun. Wieland, the happy Wieland, the adopted child of every muse, the favorite pupil of the graces, formed the powers of his extraordinary mind in a lonely and obscure retreat, the little village of Biberach, in the circle of Suabia, and thereby laid the foundation for that indisputable glory he has since attained. In solitude and silence he enriched his mind with all the stores that art and science could produce, and enabled himself to delight and instruct mankind, by adorning the sober mien of philosophy, and the lively smiles of wit, with the true spirit and irresistible charms of poetry. Retirement is the true parent of the great and good, and the kind nurse of nature's powers. It is to occasional retirement that politics owe the ablest statesmen, and philosophy the most celebrated sages. Did Aristotle, the peripatetic chief, compose his profound systems in the tumultuous court of Philip, or were the sublime theories of his master conceived among the noisy feasts of the tyrant Dionysius? No. The celebrated groves of the Academy, and the shades of Atarnya, bear witness of the important advantages which, in the opinion of both Plato and Aristotle, learning may derive from a rational retirement. These great men, like all others who preceded or have followed them, found in the ease and quietude of retirement the best means of forming their minds and extending their discoveries. The celebrated Leibnitz, to whom the world is deeply indebted, passed a great part of every year at an humble, quiet, retired, and beautiful villa which he possessed in the vicinity of Hanover.

To this catalogue of causes, conducing to a love of solitude, or hatred of society, we may add religion and fanaticism. The benign genius of religion leads the mind to a love of retirement from motives the highest, the most noble, and most really interesting, that can possibly be conceived, and produces the most perfect state of human happiness, by instilling into the heart the most virtuous propensities, and inspiring the mind with its finest energies: but fanaticism must ever be unhappy: for it proceeds from a subversion of nature itself, is formed on a perversion of reason, and a violation of truth; it is the vice of low and little understandings, is produced by an ignorance of human nature, a misapprehension of the Deity, and cannot be practised without renunciation of real virtue. The passion of retirement, which a sense of religion enforces, rises in proportion as the heart is pure, and the mind correct; but the disposition to solitude, which fanaticism creates, arises from a wild enthusiastic notion of inspiration, and increases in proportion as the heart is corrupt, and the mind deranged. Religion is the offspring of truth and love, and the parent of benevolence, hope, and joy: but the monster fanaticism is the child of discontent, and her followers are fear and sorrow. Religion is not confined to cells and closets, nor restrained to sullen retirement; these are the gloomy retreats of fanaticism, by which she endeavors to break those chains of benevolence and social affection that link the welfare of every individual with that of the whole. The greatest honor we can pay to the Author of our being, is such a cheerful behavior as discovers a mind satisfied with his dispensations. But this temper of mind is most likely to be attained by a rational retirement from the cares and pleasures of the world.

The disposition to solitude, however, of whatever kind or complexion it may be, is greatly influenced by the temper and constitution of the body, as well as by the frame and turn of the mind. The action of those causes proceeds, perhaps, by slow and insensible degrees, and varies in its form and manner in each individual; but though gradual or multiform, it at length reaches its point, and confirms the subject of it in habits of rational retreat, or unnatural solitude.

The motives which conduce to a love of solitude might, without doubt, be assigned to other causes; but a discussion of all the refined operations to which the mind may be exposed, and its bent and inclination determined, by the two great powers of sensation and reflection, would be more curious than useful. Relinquishing all inquiry into the primary or remote causes of human action, to those who are fond of the useless subtilties of metaphysics, and confining our researches to those final or immediate causes which produce this disposition to enjoy the benefits of rational retirement, or encounter the mischiefs of irrational solitude, we shall proceed to show the mischiefs which may result from the one, in order that they may be contrasted with the advantages which, in the first part, we have already shown may be derived from the other.

Chapter III
The disadvantages of solitude

The retirement which is not the result of cool and deliberate reason, so far from improving the feelings of the heart, or strengthening the powers of the mind, generally renders men less able to discharge the duties and endure the burdens of life. The wisest and best formed system of retirement is, indeed, surrounded with a variety of dangers, which are not, without the greatest care and caution, easily avoided. But in every species of total solitude, the perils are not only innumerable, but almost irresistible. It would, however, be erroneous to impute all the defects which may characterize such a recluse merely to the loneliness of his situation. There are original defects implanted by the hand of nature in every constitution, which no species of retirement and discipline can totally eradicate: there are certain vices, the seeds of which are so inherent, that no care, however great, can totally destroy. The advantages or disadvantages arising from retirement, will always be proportionate to the degrees of virtue and vice which prevail in the character of the recluse. It is certain that an occasional retreat from the business of the world will greatly improve the virtues, and increase the happiness, of him on whom nature has bestowed a sound understanding and a sensible heart; but when the heart is corrupt, the understanding weak, the imagination flighty, and the disposition depraved, solitude only tends to increase the evil and to render the character more rank and vicious; for whatever be the culture, the produce will unavoidably partake of the quality of the seeds and the nature of the soil; and solitude, by allowing a weak and wicked mind leisure to brood over its own suggestions, recreates and rears the mischief it was intended to prevent.

"… Where solitude, sad nurse of care,

To sickly musing gives the pensive mind,

There madness enters: and the dim-eyed fiend,

Lorn melancholy, night and day provokes

Her own eternal wound. The sun grows pale;

A mournful visionary light o'erspreads

The cheerful face of nature; earth becomes

A dreary desert; and the heavens frown above.

The various shapes of cursed illusion rise;

Whate'er the wretched fear, creating fear

Forms out of nothing; and with monsters teems

Unknown in hell. The prostrate soul beneath

A load of huge imagination heaves:

And all the horrors that the guilty feel,

With anxious flutterings wake the guilty breast.

From other cares absolved, the busy mind

Finds in itself a theme to pore upon;

And finds it miserable, or makes it so."

To enable the mind, however, to form an accurate judgment of the probable consequences of solitude, it is, perhaps, necessary to have seen instances both of its advantageous and detrimental effects. The consequences vary with the subject on which it operates; and the same species of solitude which to one character would be injurious, will prove to another of the highest benefit and advantage. The same person, indeed, may at different periods, as his disposition changes, experience, under similar circumstances of retirement, very different effects. Certain, however, it is, that an occasional retreat from the tumultuous intercourses of society, or a judicious and well arranged retirement, cannot be prejudicial. To have pointed out the train of virtues it is capable of producing, and to have been silent upon the black catalogue of vices that may result from extreme seclusion, would have been the more pleasing task; but I have undertaken to draw the character of solitude impartially, and must therefore point out its possible defects.

Man in a sate of solitary indolence and inactivity, sinks by degrees like stagnant water into impurity and corruption. The body suffers with the mind's decay. It is more fatal than excess of action. It is a malady that renders every hope of recovery vain and visionary. To sink from action into rest, is only indulging the common course of nature; but to rise from long continued indolence to voluntary activity, is extremely difficult, and almost impracticable. A celebrated poet has finely described this class of unhappy beings in the following lines:

"Then look'd, and saw a lazy lolling sort,

Unseen at church, at senate, or at court,

Of ever listless loiterers, that attend

No cause, no trust, no duty, and no friend.

Thee, too, my Paridel! she mark'd thee there,

Stretch'd on the rack of a too easy chair,

And heard the everlasting yawn confess

The pains and penalties of idleness."

To preserve the proper strength, both of the body and the mind, labor must be regularly and seasonably mingled with rest. Each of them require their suited exercise and relaxations. Philosophers, who aim at the attainment of every superior excellency, do not indulge themselves in ease, and securely and indolently wait for the cruelties of fortune to attack them in their retirement; but, for fear she should surprise them in the state of inexperienced and raw soldiers, undisciplined for the battle they sally out to meet her, and put themselves into regular training, and even upon the proof of hardships. Those only who observe a proper interchange of exercise and rest, can expect to enjoy health of body, or cheerfulness of mind. It is the only means by which the economy of the human frame can be regularly preserved.

He, therefore, who does not possess sufficient activity to keep the body and mind in proper exercise; he who is unacquainted with the art of varying his amusements, of changing the subjects of his contemplation, and of finding within himself all the materials of enjoyment, will soon feel solitude not only burdensome, but insupportable. To such a character, solitude will not only be disagreeable, but dangerous; for the moment the temporary passion which draws him from society has subsided, he will sink into languor and indifference; and this temper is always unfavorable to moral sentiment. The world, perhaps, with all its disadvantages, is less likely to be injurious to such a man, than the calm and silent shades of unenjoyed retirement.

Solitude also, particularly when carried to an extreme, is apt to render the character of the recluse rigid, austere, and inflexible, and of course, unsuited to the enjoyments of society. The notions he contracts are as singular and abstracted as his situation: he adheres to them with inflexible pertinacity: his mind moves only in the accustomed track: he cherishes his preconceived errors and prejudices with fond attachment, and despises those whose sentiments are contrary to his own. A promiscuous intercourse with society has the effect of rendering the mind docile, and his judgment of men and things correct: for in the world every subject is closely examined, every question critically discussed; and, while the spirit of controversy and opposition elicits truth, the mind is led into a train of rational investigation, and its powers strengthened and enlarged; but the mind of the recluse being uninterruptedly confined to its own course of reasoning, and to the habit of viewing objects on one side, it is unable to appreciate the respective weights which different arguments may deserve, or to judge in doubtful cases, on which side, truth is most likely to be found. A commixture of different opinions, on any particular subject, provokes a free and liberal discussion of it, an advantage which the prepossession engendered by solitude uniformly prevents.

Solitude, while it establishes a dangerous confidence in the powers and opinions of its votaries, not only fastens on the characters the errors and imperfections it has produced and fostered, but recommends them strongly to their esteem. How frequently do we observe, even in persons of rank and fortune, who reside continually on their own estates, a haughty manner and arbitrary disposition, totally incompatible with that candid conduct, that open minded behavior, that condescending urbanity, that free spirit, which mark the character of the polite and liberal minded gentleman, and render him the veneration and delight of all around him! "Obstinacy and pride," says Plato, "are the inevitable consequences of a solitary life;" and the frequency of the fact certainly justifies the observation. Retired, secluded characters, having no opportunity of encountering the opinions of others, or of listening to any other judgment than their own, establish a species of tyranny over their understandings, and check that free excursion of the intellect which the discovery of truth requires. They reject, with disdain, the close investigations of logic, and repel all attempts to examine their arguments, and expose their fallacies. Their preconceived opinions, which they dignify with the appellation of settled truths, and mistake for indisputable axioms, have infixed themselves so deeply in their minds that they cannot endure the idea of their being rooted out or removed: and they are fearful of submitting them to the test of controversy, only because they were originally received without due examination, and have been confirmed by the implicit consent and approbation of their inferiors and dependants.

Solitude also, even the solitude which poets and philosophers have so feelingly described as blissful and beneficial, has frequently proved injurious to its delighted votaries. Men of letters are, in general, too inattentive to those easy and captivating manners which give such high spirit to the address, and splendid decoration to the characters, of well bred men. They seldom qualify the awkwardness of scholastic habits by a free and intimate intercourse either with the world or with each other; but being secluded from society, and engaged in abstracted pursuits, adopt a pedantic phraseology, an unaccommodating address, formal notions, and a partial attachment to their recondite pursuits. The common topics of conversation, and usual entertainment of company, they treat with high, but unjustifiable disdain; and, blinded by fogs of pride, and ideal superiority, are rendered incapable of discerning their errors.

The correction of this disposition in authors has been thought of so much importance to the interests of morals, and to the manners of the rising generation, that scholars in general have been exhorted, in the highest strains of eloquence, by one of the most powerful preachers of Germany, from the pulpit of the politest city in the empire, to guard with unceasing vigilance against those defects which are so apt to mingle with the habits of the profession, and which tend to sully the brightness of their characters. The orator invokes them to shake off that distant demeanor, that unsocial reserve, that supercilious behavior and almost express contempt, from which few of them are free, and which most of them practise when in unlettered company; and to treat their fellow citizens, however inferior they may be in erudition and scholastic knowledge, with affability and attention; to listen to their conversation with politeness; to regard their errors with lenity; to view their failings with compassion, and their defects with liberality; to lead them into the paths of truth and science by mild persuasion, to lure them to knowledge by gentle means, and, by reducing their conversation and subjects of discourse to a level with the unlettered understandings of their auditors, to please the heart while they instruct the mind.

> Good sense and learning may esteem obtain,
>
> Humor and wit a laugh, if rightly ta'en:
>
> Fair virtue admiration may impart;
>
> But 'tis good nature only wins the heart:
>
> It moulds the body to an easy grace,
>
> And brightens every feature of the face:
>
> It smooths th' unpolish'd tongue with eloquence,
>
> And adds persuasion to the finest sense.

Learning and good sense, indeed, to whatever degree they may be possessed, can only render the possessor happy in proportion as he employs them to increase the happiness of others. To effect this, he must occasionally endure the jokes of dullness without petulance, and listen with complacency to the observations of ignorance, but, above all, he must carefully avoid all inclination to exhibit his own superiority, and to shine at the expense of others.

Learning and wisdom, indeed, however they may be confounded by arrogant and self-conceited scholars, are in no respects synonymous terms; but, on the contrary, are not unfrequently quite at variance with each other.

The high admiration which scholars are too apt to entertain of the excellency of their own talents, and the vast importance they generally ascribe to their own characters and merit, instead of producing that sound judgment upon men and things which constitutes true wisdom, only engenders an effervescence in the imagination, the effect of which is in general, the most frothy folly. Many of those who thus pride themselves on the pursuits of literature, having nothing to boast of but an indefatigable attention to some idle and unprofitable study; a study which, perhaps only tends to contract the feelings of the heart, and impoverish the powers of the mind. True wisdom and genuine virtue are the produce of those enlarged views which arise from a general and comprehensive knowledge both of books and men: but scholars, who confine their attention entirely to books, and feel no interest or concern for the world, despise every object that does not lie within the range of their respective studies. By poring over obsolete works, they acquire sentiments quite foreign to the manners of the age in which we live; form opinions as ridiculous as they are unfashionable; fabricate systems incomprehensible to the rest of mankind; and maintain arguments so offensive and absurd, that whenever they venture to display their acquirements in society, they are, like the bird of night, hooted back with derision into their daily obscurity. Many studious characters are so puffed up by arrogance, presumption, self-conceit, and vanity, that they can scarcely speak upon any subject without hurting the feelings of their friends and giving cause of triumph to their enemies. The counsel and instruction they affect to give is so mixed with ostentatious pedantry, that they destroy the very end they wish to promote: and, instead of acquiring honorable approbation, cover themselves with merited disgrace. Plato, the illustrious chief of the academic set of Athenian philosophers was so totally free from this vice of inferior minds, that it was impossible to discover in him by ordinary and casual conversation, that sublime imagination and almost divine intellect, which rendered him the idol of his age, and the admiration of succeeding generations. On his return from Syracuse, to which place he had been invited by Dionysius the younger, he visited Olympia, to be present at the performance of the Olympic games; and he was placed on the seat appropriated to foreigners of the highest distinction, but to whom he was not personally known. Some of them were so pleased with the ease, politeness, wisdom, and vivacity of his conversation, that they accompanied him to Athens, and, on their arrival in that city, requested him to procure them an interview with Plato. But how pleasing and satisfactory was their surprise, when, on his replying with a smile, *"I am the person whom you wish to see,"* they discovered that this affable and entertaining companion, with whom they had travelled without discerning his excellency, was the most learned and profound philosopher at that time existing in the world! The studious and retired life of this extraordinary character had not decreased his urbanity and politeness, nor deprived him of the exercise of those easy and seducing manners which so entirely engage the affection and win the heart. He wisely prevented seclusion from robbing him of that amenity and unassuming ease so necessary to the enjoyment of society. Like those two eminent philosophers of the present day, the wise Mendelsohm, and the amiable Garve, he derived from solitude all the benefits it is capable of conferring, without suffering any of those injuries which it too frequently inflicts on less powerful minds.

Culpable, however, as studious characters in general are, by neglecting to cultivate that social address, and to observe that civility of manners, and urbane attention, which an intercourse not only with the world, but even with private society, so indispensably requires, certain it is, that men of fashion expect from them a more refined good breeding, and a nicer attention to the forms of politeness, than all their endeavors can produce. The fashionable world, indeed, are blamable for their constant attempts to deride the awkwardness of their more erudite and abstracted companions. The severity with which they treat the defective manners of a scholastic visitor, is a violation of the first rules of true politeness, which consists entirely of a happy combination of good sense and good nature, both of which dictate a different conduct, and induce rather a friendly concealment than a triumphant exposure of such venial failings. The inexperienced scholastic is entitled to indulgence, for he cannot be expected nicely to practice customs which he has had no opportunity to learn. To the eye of polished life, his austerity, his reserve, his mistakes, his indecorums, may, perhaps, appear ridiculous; but to expose him to derision on this subject is destructive to the general interests of society, inasmuch as it tends to repress and damp endeavors to please. How is it possible that men who devote the greater portion of their time to the solitary and abstracted pursuits of literature, can possess that promptitude of thought, that variety of expression, those easy manners, and that varying humor, which prevail so agreeably in mixed society, and which can only be acquired by a constant intercourse with the world? It was not only cruel, but unjust, of the Swedish courtiers to divert themselves with the confusion and embarrassments into which Miebom and Naude, two celebrated writers on the music and dances of the ancients were thrown, when the celebrated Christina desired the one to sing and the other to dance in public, for the entertainment of the court. Still less excusable were those imps of fashion in France, who exposed the celebrated mathematician, Nicole, to the derision of a large company, for the misapplication of a word. A fashionable female at Paris, having heard that Nicole, who had then lately written a profound and highly approved treatise on the doctrine of curves, was greatly celebrated in all the circles of science, and affecting to be thought the patroness and intimate of all persons of distinguished merit, sent him such an invitation to one of her parties that he could not refuse to accept of. The abstracted geometrician, who had never before been present at an assembly of the kind, received the civilities of his fair hostess, and her illustrious friends, with all the awkwardness and confusion which such a scene must naturally create. After passing an uncomfortable evening, in answering the observations of those who addressed him, in which he experienced much greater difficulties than he would have found in solving the most intricate problem, he prepared to take his leave, and pouring out a profusion of declarations to the lady of the house, of the grateful sense he entertained of the high honor she had conferred on him, by her generous invitation, distinguishing attention, polite regard, and extraordinary civility, rose to the climax of his compliments, by assuring her, that the *lovely little eyes of his fair entertainer had made an impression which never could be erased from his breast*, and immediately departed. But a kind friend, who was accompanying him home, whispering in his ear, as they were passing the stairs, that he had paid the lady a very ill compliment, by telling her that her eyes were little, for that little eyes were universally understood by the whole sex to be a great defect. Nicole, mortified to an extreme by the mistake he had thus innocently made, and resolving to apologize to the lady whom he conceived he had offended, returned abruptly to the company, and entreated her with great humility, to pardon the error into which his confusion had betrayed him of imputing any thing like *littleness* to so high, so elegant, so distinguished a character, declaring that he had never beheld *such fine large eyes, such fine large lips, such fine large hands, or so fine and large a person altogether*, in the whole course of his life!

The professional pursuits of students confine them, during the early periods of life, to retirement and seclusion, and prevent them in general, from attempting to mix in the society of the world until age, or professional habits, have rendered them unfit for this scene. Discouraged by the neglect they experience, and by the ridicule to which they are exposed, on their first introduction into active life, from persevering in their attempts to shake off the uncouth manner they have acquired, they immediately shrink from the displeasing prospect into their original obscurity, in despair of ever attaining the talents necessary to render them agreeable to the elegant and gay. There are, indeed, some men, who, on attempting to change the calm and rational enjoyments of a retired and studious life, for the more lively and loquacious pleasures of public society, perceive the manners and maxims of the world so repugnant to their principles, and so disagreeable to their taste and inclinations, that they instantly abandon society, and, renouncing all future attempts to enter into its vortex, calmly and contentedly return to their beloved retreat under an idea that it is wrong for persons of such different dispositions to intermix or invade the provinces of each other. There are also many studious characters who avoid society, under an idea that they have transferred their whole minds into their own compositions; that they have exhausted all that they possessed of either instruction or entertainment; and that they would, like empty bottles, or squeezed oranges, be thrown aside with disregard, and, perhaps, with contempt, as persons no longer capable of contributing to companionable pleasures. But there are others of sounder sense and better judgment, who gladly relinquish the noisy assemblies of public life, and joyfully retire to the sweet and tranquil scenes of rural solitude, because they seldom meet among the candidates for public approbation, a single individual capable of enjoying a just thought, or making a rational reflection; but, on the contrary, have to encounter a host of vain, frivolous pretenders to wit and learning, who herd together, like the anarchs of insurrection, to oppose with noise and violence, the progress of truth and the exertions of reason.

Sentiments like these too frequently banish from the circles of society characters of useful knowledge and of distinguished genius, and from whose endowments mankind might receive both instruction and delight. The loss, in such a case, to the individual is, perhaps, trifling; his comforts may possibly be increased by his seclusion; but the interests of truth and good sense are thereby considerably injured: for the mind of man, however powerful and informed it may be in itself, cannot employ its energies and acquisitions with the same advantage and effect, as when it is whetted by a collision with other minds, and polished by the manners of the world. An acquaintance with the living characters and manners of the world, teaches the mind to direct its powers to their proper and most useful points: exhibits the means and furnishes the instruments, by which the best exertions of virtue can attain her ends; gives morals their brightest color, taste its highest refinement, and truth its fairest objects. The wisest and best philosophers have acknowledged the obligations they were under to society for the knowledge they acquired in its extensive, though dangerous school, and have strongly recommended the study of mankind, by viewing all the various classes with a discriminating eye, as the best means of becoming acquainted with the beauties of *virtue*, and the deformities of *vice*, and, of course, as the best means of discovering the true road to earthly happiness; for—

> Virtue, immortal virtue! born to please,
> The child of nature and the source of ease,

Bids every bliss on human life attend;

To every rank a kind and faithful friend;

Inspirits nature 'midst the scenes of toil,

Smooths languor's cheek, and bids fell want recoil:

Shines from the mitre with unsullied rays,

Glares on the crest, and gives the star to blaze;

Supports distinction, spreads ambition's wings,

Forms saints of queens, and demi-gods of kings;

O'er grief, oppression, envy, scorn, prevails,

And makes a cottage greater than Versailles.

A free, open, unconstrained intercourse with mankind, has also the advantage of reconciling us to the peculiarities of others, and of teaching us the important lesson how to accommodate our minds and manners to such principles, opinions, and dispositions, as may differ from our own. The learned and enlightened cannot maintain an intercourse with the illiterate, without exercising an extraordinary degree of patience, conceding many points which appear unnatural, and forbearing to feel those little vexations so adherent to characters who have lived in retirement. The philosopher, in order to teach virtue to the world with any hope of success, must humor its vices to a certain degree, and sometimes even adopt the follies he intends to destroy. To inculcate wisdom, it is necessary to follow the examples of Socrates and Wieland, and, separating from morals all that is harsh, repulsive, and anti-social, adopt only the kind and complacent tenets of the science. A German author of the present day, whom I glory to call both my countryman and my friend, observes, with the sagacity and discrimination of a critic, in his "Remarks on the Writings and Genius of Franklin," that the compositions of that great and extraordinary character are totally free from that pomp of style and parade of erudition, which so frequently disfigure the writings of other authors, and defeat their intended effect. The pen of Franklin renders the most abstract principles easy and familiar. He conveys his instructions in pleasing narrations, lively adventures, or humorous observations; and while his manner wins upon the heart, by the friendly interest he appears to take in the concerns of mankind, his matter instils into the mind the soundest principles of morals and good policy. He makes fancy the handmaid to reason in her researches into science, and penetrates the understanding through the medium of the affections. A secret charm pervades every part of his works. He rivets the attention by the strength of his observations, and relieves it by the variety of pleasing images with which he embellishes his subject. The perspicuity of his style, and the equally easy and eloquent turn of his periods, give life and energy to his thoughts; and, while the reader feels his heart bounding with delight, he finds his mind impregnated with instruction. These high advantages resulted entirely from his having studied the world, and gained an accurate knowledge of mankind. An author, indeed, may acquire an extraordinary fund of knowledge in solitude; but it is in society alone that he can learn how to render it useful. Before he can instruct the world, he must be enabled to view its fooleries and vices with calm inspection; to contemplate them without anger, as the unavoidable consequences of human infirmity; to treat them with tenderness; and to avoid exasperating the feelings of those whose depravity he is attempting to correct. A moral censor whose disposition is kind and benevolent, never suffers his superior virtue, knowledge, or talents, however great they may be, to offend the feelings of others; but, like Socrates, he will appear as if he were receiving himself the instruction he is imparting. It is a fine observation of the celebrated Goethe, that kindness is the golden chain by which society is bound together: those who have had the happiness to converse with that extraordinary man, must have perceived the anxiety with which he endeavors to temper the strength of his genius by the mildness and amenity of his conversation.

Men of letters, however awkward the habits of seclusion may have rendered them, would, I am convinced, be, in general, if not always, treated with great politeness and attention, if they would be careful to treat others with the common candor which humanity requires, and with that indulgence and affability which true liberality of sentiment will ever dictate; but how few, alas! are there who, by complacency and condescension, entitle themselves to the kindness and civility of which they stand so much in need, and so arrogantly expect! How is it possible for those who are vigilantly anxious to depress the rising merit of others, ever to gain their friendship or esteem? Friendship can only be acquired by an open, sincere, liberal, and manly conduct; but he whose breast is filled with envy and jealousy, who cautiously examines, before he speaks, every sentiment and feeling, lest his tongue should betray the meanness of his heart, and the poverty of his mind; who seizes every light indiscretion, or trifling error, that many inadvertently escape from his companions; who silently repines at every excellency, both moral and intellectual, which they may discover; who, even when surrounded by those who wish him well, continues with guarded circumspection, and suspicious caution, to weigh the motives of their actions and conversation, as if he were surrounded by the bitterest enemies, must be utterly incapable of esteeming others, or being esteemed himself; and to suppose that the generous flame of friendship, that holy fire which, under the deepest adversity, so comfortably warms and cheers the heart, can ever spring up from such cold materials, and ashy embers, would be extravagant and ridiculous.

The delight which the heart experiences in pouring forth the fulness of its feelings, with honest confidence, into the bosom of a faithful friend, is permanent and unbounded. The pleasures which spring from the acquisition of fame, whether resulting from the generous voice of an approving public, or extorted from the reluctant tongues of envious rivals and contemporaries, will bear no comparison with those which thrill through the exulting bosom of him who can justly exclaim, "To the heart of this unhappy man I have given returning hopes, and made him look forward with confidence to the enjoyment of peace; to his wounded spirit I have imparted the balm of comfort and tranquillity; and from the bleeding bosom of my friend have driven despair!" But to perform such offices as these, it is indispensably necessary that we should have recommended ourselves to the confidence, and have gained the affections of those we intend to serve. This great and necessary property, however, those who live secluded lives very seldom possess: but, much as they may in general disdain to practise this high virtue, it is necessary that they should know that it tends more to ennoble the sentiments of the mind, and to raise the feelings of the heart, than their most successful researches to discover something before unheard of in the regions of science, and which they pursue with as much avidity as if truth were liable to decay, unless sustained by the aid of novelty.

It is justly and beautifully said by one of the apocryphal writers, that *a faithful friend is the medicine of life*. A variety of occasions happen, when to pour forth the heart to one whom we love and trust, is the chief comfort, perhaps the only relief we can enjoy. Miserable is he who, shut up within the narrow inclosure of selfish interest, has no person to whom he can at all times, with full confidence, expand his soul. But he who can only feel an affection for such as listen continually to the suggestions of vanity, as applaud indiscriminately the imaginary prodigies of his wit, or never contradict the egotism of his opinions, is totally unfit for friendship, and utterly unworthy of respect. It is men of learning and of retired habits, who are most likely to adopt this disengaging disposition. There are, I am sorry to say it, many men, distinguished in the paths of science, who affect to possess the most refined sensibility, and whose tongues are continually proclaiming the virtues of benevolence, but who, when they are called upon to practise those virtues in behalf of some distressed companion, turn a deaf ear to the appeal, form some poor excuse for not interfering, and, if pressed to come forward with some promised assistance, deny to afford it, because the unhappy sufferer has neglected to approve of some extravagant conjecture, or to adopt all the visionary notions and Utopian systems they may have framed. He who neglects to perform the common charities of life, because his idle vanity may have been offended by the neglect or indifference of his companions, will never find, and cannot become, a real friend. There is also an inferior order of fops in literature, (if any order can be inferior to that which I have last described,) who carry with them, wherever they go, a collection of their latest compositions, and by importunately reading them to every one they meet, and expecting an unreserved approbation of their merits, render themselves so unpleasantly troublesome on all occasions that, instead of conciliating the least regard or esteem, their very approach is dreaded as much as a pestilence or a famine. Every man of real genius will shun this false ambition of gratifying vanity by forced applause; because he will immediately perceive, that instead of gaining the hearts of his auditors, he only exposes himself to the ridicule, and loses all chance of their esteem.

The disadvantages, however, which studious characters have been described to experience from habits of solitary seclusion, and by neglecting the manners of society, must not be indiscriminately applied. It is the morose and surly pedant, who sits silently in his solitary study, and endeavors to enforce a character for genius in opposition to nature, who adopts the mean and unworthy arts of jealousy, suspicion, and dishonest praise. Far different the calm, happy, and honorable life of him who, devoted to the cultivation of a strong understanding, and the improvement of a feeling heart, is enabled, by his application and genius, to direct the taste of the age by his liberality of spirit, to look on his equals without jealousy, and his superiors with admiration; and, by his benevolence, to feel for the multitude he instructs, indulgence and affection; who, relying on the real greatness of his temper, makes no attempt to increase his importance by low raillery or unfounded satire; whose firm temper never sinks into supine indolence, or grovelling melancholy; who only considers his profession as the means of meliorating mankind; who perseveres in the cause of truth with cheerful rectitude, and virtuous dignity; whose intellectual resources satisfactorily supply the absence of society; whose capacious mind enables him to increase his stores of useful knowledge; whose discriminating powers enable him to elucidate the subject he explores; who feels as great a delight in promoting the beneficial discoveries of others, as in executing his own; and who regards his professional contemporaries, not as jealous rivals, but as generous friends, striving to emulate each other in the noble pursuits of science, and in the laudable task of endeavoring to improve the morals of mankind.

Characters of this description, equally venerable and happy, are numerous in Europe, both within and without the shades of academic bowers, and afford examples which, notwithstanding the tribe of errors and absurdities solitude occasionally engenders, should induce men of worldly pleasures to repress the antipathies they are in general inclined to feel against persons of studious and retired lives.

Chapter IV
The influence of solitude on the imagination

The powers of imagination are great; and the effects produced by them, under certain circumstances, upon the minds of men of warm and sensible tempers, extraordinary and surprising. Multitudes have been induced by perturbed imaginations, to abandon the gay and cheerful haunts of men, and to seek, in dreary desolation, comfort and repose. To such extremes has this faculty, when distorted, hurried its unhappy subjects, that they have endured the severest mortification, denied themselves the common benefits of nature, exposed themselves to the keenest edge of winter's cold, and the most scorching rays of summer's heat, and indulged their distempered fancies in the wildest chimeras. These dreadful effects appear, on a first view, to be owing to some supernatural cause, and they agitate our senses, and confuse the understanding, as phenomena beyond the comprehension of reason; but the wonder vanishes when the cause is coolly and carefully explored; and the extravagances are traced up to their real source, and natural organization of man. The wild ideas of the hermit Anthony, who, in his gloomy retreat, fancied that Beelzebub appeared to him in the form of a beautiful female to torture his senses, and disturb his repose, originated in his natural character and disposition. His distempered fancy conjured up a fiend, which, in fact, existed in his unsubdued passions and incontinent desires.

> … From the enchanting cup
>
> Which fancy holds to all, the unwary thirst
>
> Of youth oft swallows a Circæan draught,
>
> That sheds a baleful tincture o'er the eye
>
> Of reason, till no longer he discerns,
>
> And only lives to err: then revel forth
>
> A furious band, that spurn him from the throne,
>
> And all is uproar. Hence the fevered heart
>
> Pants with delirious hope for tinsel charms.

Solitude excites and strengthens the powers of the imagination to an uncommon degree, and thereby enfeebles the effect of the controlling powers of reason. The office of the latter faculty of the mind is, to examine with nice discernment and scrupulous attention, to compare the several properties of thoughts and things with each other, and to acquire, by cool and deliberate investigation, correct ideas of their combinations and effects. The exercise of their power suspends the vehemence of action, and abates the ardor of desire; but fancy performs her airy excursions upon light and vagrant wings, and flying around her objects without examination, embraces every pleasing image with increasing delight. Judgment separates and associates the ideas the mind has gained by sensation and reflection, and by determining their agreement or disagreement, searches after truth through the medium of probability; but the imagination employs itself in raising unsubstantial images, and portraying the form of things unknown in nature, and foreign to truth. It has, indeed, like memory, the power of reviving in the mind the ideas which, after having been imprinted there, have disappeared; but it differs from that faculty by altering, enlarging, diversifying, and frequently distorting, the subjects of its power.

> It bodies forth the form of things unknown,
>
> And gives to airy nothings
>
> A local habitation and a name.

But the irregular and wild desires which seize upon the mind through the avenues of an untamed fancy and disordered imagination, are not exclusively the produce of solitude. The choice of wisdom or folly is offered to us in all places, and under every circumstance; but the mind of man is unhappily prone to that which is least worthy of it. I shall therefore endeavor to show, by some general observations, in what instances solitude is most likely to create those flights of imagination which mislead the mind, and corrupt the heart.

Imagination is said to be the simple apprehension of corporeal objects when they are absent; which absence of the object it contemplates, distinguishes this faculty from *sensation*, and has occasioned some metaphysicians to call it *recorded sensation*. Upon the due regulation, and proper management, of this great and extraordinary power of the mind, depends, in a great measure, the happiness or misery of life. It ought to consist of a happy combination of those ideas we receive through the organs of bodily sense, and those which we derive from the faculties of moral perception; but it too frequently consists of a capricious and ill-formed mixture of heterogeneous images, which though true in themselves, are false in the way they are applied. Thus a person, the circulation of whose blood in any particular member is suddenly stopped, *imagines* that needles are pricking the disordered part. The sensation in this case is real, but the conclusion from it is fallacious. So in every mental illusion, imagination, when she first begins to exercise her powers, seizes on some fact, of the real nature of which the mind has but an obscure idea, and, for want of tracing it through all its connexions and dependences, misleads reason into the darkest paths of error. The wild conjectures, and extravagant opinions which have issued from this source are innumerable. The imagination receives every impulse with eagerness, while the passions crowd around her splendid throne, obedient to her dictates. They act, indeed, reciprocally on each other. The imagination pours a concourse of contrary ideas into the mind, and easily disregards, or reconciles their incongruities. The voice of the calm inquirer, reason, is incapable of being heard amidst the tumult; and the favorite image is animated and enlarged by the glowing fire of the passions. No power remains to control or regulate, much less to subdue, this mental ray, which inflames the whole soul, and exalts it into the fervor of enthusiasm, hurries it into the extravagance of superstition: or precipitates it into the furious frenzies of fanaticism.

> The powerful tumult reigns in every part,
>
> Pants in the breast, and swells the rising heart.

Enthusiasm is that ecstacy of the mind, that lively transport of the soul, which is excited by the pursuit or contemplation of some great and noble object, the novelty of which awakens attention, the truth of which fixes the understanding, and the grandeur of which, by firing the fancy, engages the aid of every passion, and prompts the mind to the highest undertakings. A just and rightly formed enthusiasm is founded in reason, and supported by nature, and carries the mind above its ordinary level, into the unexplored regions of art and science. The rational enthusiast, indeed, rises to an elevation so far above the distinct view of vulgar eyes, that common understandings are apt to treat him either with blind admiration, or cool contempt, only because they are incapable of comprehending his real character; and while some bow to him as an extraordinary genius, others rail at him as an unhappy lunatic. The powers of enthusiasm, however, when founded upon proper principles, so strengthen and invigorate the faculties of the mind, as to enable it to resist danger undismayed, and to surmount difficulties that appear irresistible. Those, indeed, who have possessed themselves of this power to any extraordinary degree, have been considered as *inspired*, and their great achievements conceived to have been directed by councils, and sustained by energies of a divine or super-mundane nature. Certain it is, that we owe to the spirit of enthusiasm whatever is great in art, sublime in science, or noble in the human character: and the elegant and philosophic

Lord Shaftsbury, while he ridicules the absurdities of this wonderfully powerful and extensive quality, admits that it is impossible to forbear ascribing to it whatever is greatly performed by heroes, statesmen, poets, orators, and even philosophers themselves: and who that is not contented to wallow in the mire of gross sensuality, would not quit the noisy scenes of tumultuous dissipation, and repair with joy and gladness to solitary shades, to the bower of tranquillity, and the fountain of peace, to majestic forests, and to verdant groves, to acquire this necessary ingredient to perfect excellence? Who would not willingly pierce the pensive gloom, or dwell among the brighter glories of the golden age, to acquire by a warm and glowing, but correct and chaste contemplation of the beautiful and sublime works of nature, these ravishing sensations, and gain this noble fervor of the imagination? A proper study of the works of nature amidst the romantic scenery of sylvan solitude, is certainly the most likely means of inspiring the mind with true enthusiasm, and leading genius to her most exalted heights; but the attempt is dangerous. There are few men in whose minds airy notions do not sometimes tyrannize. "To indulge the power of fiction," says a celebrated writer, "and send imagination out upon the wing, is often the sport of those who delight too much in silent speculation. When we are alone, we are not always busy; the labor of excogitation is too violent to last long; the ardor of inquiry will sometimes give way to idleness or satiety. He who has nothing external that can divert him, must find pleasure in his own thoughts, and must conceive himself what he is not; for who is pleased with what he is? He then expatiates in boundless futurity, and culls from all imaginable conditions that which for the present moment he should most desire, amuses his desires with impossible enjoyments, and confers upon his pride unattainable dominion. The mind dances from scene to scene, unites all pleasures in all combinations, riots in delights which nature and fortune, with all their bounty, cannot bestow. In time some particular train of ideas fixes the attention; all other intellectual gratifications are rejected; the mind in weariness or leisure, recurs constantly to the favorite conception, and feasts on the luscious falsehood whenever she is offended with the bitterness of truth. By degrees the reign of fancy is confirmed; she grows first imperious, and in time despotic: then fictions begin to operate as realities, false opinions fasten on the mind, and life passes in dreams of rapture or of anguish. This is one of the dangers of solitude."

These observations lead us to consider the character of the fanatical visionary, who feels, like the happy enthusiast, the same agitation of passion, and the same inflammation of mind; but as the feelings of one are founded upon knowledge, truth, and nature, so the feelings of the other are the result of ignorance and error, and all the glittering meteors of his brain the effects of imposture and deception. Of this species of enthusiasm Mr. Locke gives the following description: "In all ages men in whom melancholy has mixed with devotion, or whose conceit of themselves has raised them into an opinion of a greater familiarity with God, and a nearer admittance to his favors, than is afforded to others, have often flattered themselves with a persuasion of an immediate intercourse with the Deity, and frequent communication with his divine spirit. Their minds being thus prepared, whatever groundless opinion comes to settle itself strongly upon their fancies, is an illumination from the Spirit of God, and whatever odd action they find in themselves a strong inclination to do, that impulse is concluded to be a call or direction from heaven, and must be obeyed; it is a commission from above, and they cannot err in executing it. This species of enthusiasm, though arising from the conceit of a warm and overweening brain, works, when it once gets footing, more powerfully on the persuasions and actions of men than either reason, revelation, or both together; men being forwardly obedient to all the impulses they receive from themselves." The fantastic images, indeed, which the wildness of his imagination creates, subdues his reason, and destroys the best affections of his heart, while his passions take the part of their furious assailants, and render him the victim of his visionary conceptions. It is not, however, from sources of fanatical devotion, or irrational solitude, that this vicious species of enthusiasm alone arises. The follies of faquiers, the extravagance of orgaists, the absurdities of hermits, and the mummery of monks, are not more enthusiastically injurious to the true interests of mankind, or more pregnant with all the calamitous effects of this baleful vice, than those unprincipled systems of politics and morals which have been of late years obtruded on the world, and in which good sense is sacrificed, and true science disgraced.

The growth of fanaticism, whether moral, political, religious, or scientific, is not confined exclusively to any age or country; the seeds of it have been but too plentifully sown in all the regions of the earth; and it is almost equally baneful and injurious in whatever soil they spring. Every bold, turbulent, and intriguing spirit, who has sufficient artifice to inflame the passions of the inconstant multitude, the moment he calls the demon of fanatacism to his aid, becomes troublesome, and frequently dangerous, to the government under which he lives. Even the affectation of this powerful but pernicious quality, is able to produce fermentations, highly detrimental to the peace of society. In the very metropolis of Great Britain, and among the enlightened inhabitants of that kingdom, Lord George Gordon, in the present age, was enabled, by assuming the hypocritical appearance of piety, and standing forth as a champion of a religious sect, to convulse the nation, and endanger its safety. In the twenty-first year of the reign of his Britannic

Majesty, the present powerful and illustrious King George III. an act of parliament was passed to relieve the Roman Catholics residing in England from the penalties and disabilities which had been imposed on them at the revolution. An extension of the same relief to the Catholics of Scotland was also said to be intended by parliament. The report spread an immediate alarm throughout the country; societies were formed for the defence of the Protestant faith; committees appointed, books dispersed, and, in short, every method taken to inflame the zeal of the people. These attempts being totally neglected by government, and but feebly resisted by the more liberal minded in the country, produced all their effects. A furious spirit of bigotry and persecution soon showed itself, and broke out into the most outrageous acts of violence against the Papists at Edinburgh, Glasgow, and elsewhere; but as government did not think it advisable to repress this spirit by force, the just and benevolent intentions of the legislature were laid aside. The successful resistance of the zealots in Scotland to any relaxation of the penal laws against the Papists, seems to have given the first rise to the Protestant Association in England; for about the same time bills were dispersed, and advertisements inserted in the newspapers, inviting those who wished well to the cause to unite under that title; and Lord George Gordon, who had been active at the head of the malcontents in Scotland, was chosen their President. The ferment was suffered to increase during a course of several years. His lordship was a member of the senate, and his extraordinary conduct in the house, and frequent interruption he gave to the business of parliament, as well as the unaccountable manner in which he continually brought in and treated matters relative to religion and the danger of popery, and the caprice with which he divided the house upon questions wherein he stood nearly or entirely alone, were passed over, along with other singularities in his dress and manners, rather as subjects of pleasantry than of serious notice or reprehension. On Monday, the 29th of May, 1780, a meeting was held at Coachmaker's Hall, pursuant to a public advertisement, in order to consider of the mode of presenting a petition to the House of Commons. Lord George Gordon took the chair; and, after a long inflammatory harangue, in which he endeavoured to persuade his hearers of the rapid and alarming progress that popery was making in the kingdom, he proceeded to observe, that the only way to stop it, was going in a firm, manly, and resolute manner to the house and showing their representatives that they were determined to preserve their religious freedom with their lives; that, for his part, he would run all hazards with the people; and if the people were too lukewarm to run all hazards with him, when their conscience and their country called them forth, they might get another president, for that he would tell them candidly, he was not a lukewarm man himself; and that, if they meant to spend their time in mock debate, and idle opposition, they might get another leader. This speech was received with the loudest applause, and his lordship then moved the following resolution: "That the whole body of the Protestant Association do attend in St. George's Fields, on Friday next, at ten o'clock in the morning, to accompany their president to the House of Commons at the delivery of the Protestant petition;" which was carried unanimously. His Lordship then informed them, that if less than twenty thousand of his fellow citizens attended him on that day, he would not present their petition. Accordingly, on Friday, the 2d day of June, 1780, at ten in the forenoon, several thousands assembled at the place appointed, marshalling themselves in ranks, and waiting for their leader, who arrived about an hour afterward, and they all proceeded to the houses of parliament. Here they began to exercise the most arbitrary power over both lords and commons, by obliging almost all the members to put blue cockades on their hats, and call out "no popery!" Some they compelled to take oaths to vote for the repeal of this obnoxious act; others they insulted in the most indecent and insolent manner. They took possession of all the avenues up to the very door of both houses of parliament, which they twice attempted to force open, and committed many outrages on the persons of the members. Nor were they dispersed, or the remaining members able to leave their seats, until a military force arrived. The houses were adjourned to the 19th of June. But so dreadful a spectacle of calamity and horror was never known in any age or country, as that which the metropolis of England exhibited on the evening and the day which succeeded this seditious congregation. These astonishing effects produced by the real or pretended fanaticism of a simple individual, sufficiently display the power of this dangerous quality, when artfully employed to inflame the passions of the unthinking multitude. But it is worthy of observation, that while this incendiary sustained among his followers the character of a pious patriot, of a man without the smallest spot or blemish, of being, in short, the most virtuous guardian of the established religion of the country, he regularly indulged his holy fervors, and sanctified appearances, every evening, in the company of common prostitutes, or professed wantons.

The fire of fanaticism is, indeed, so subtilely powerful, that it is capable of inflaming the coldest mind. The mildest and the most rational dispositions have been occasionally injured by its heat. The rapidity of its progress certainly depends, in a great degree, on the nature of the materials on which it acts; but, like every dangerous conflagration, its first appearances should be watched, and every means taken to extinguish its flames. The extinction is, perhaps, most happily and readily effected by those counteractions which the common occupations, and daily duties of life produce on the mind, when judiciously opposed to this flagrant evil.

Of the advantages, at least, of this resource, a circumstance in the history of the late Dr. Fothergill affords a remarkable example. This celebrated physician possessed the greatest tranquillity of mind, and had obtained so complete a dominion over his passions, that he declared to a friend, recently before his death, that he could not recollect a single instance, during the whole course of his life, in which they had been improperly disturbed. This temper, which perfectly suited to the character of the religion he professed, the tenets of which he strictly practised, he maintained on all occasions; nor was there any thing in his general conduct or manner that betrayed to his most familiar friends the least propensity toward enthusiasm; and yet, distant as the suspicion must be, under these circumstances, that he should ever be under the influence of superstition, it is well known, that while he was a student at Edinburgh, where he was distinguished for the mildness of his manners and the regularity of his conduct, he one day, in an eccentric sally of fanaticism ran, almost entirely naked through the streets of that city, warning all its inhabitants of the impending wrath of heaven; and exhorting them in the most solemn manner, to avert the approaching danger, by humbly imploring the mercy of the offended Deity; but this religious paroxysm was of short duration. He was at this time in habits of intimacy with the great characters who then filled the professional chairs of the university, and ardently engaged in the pursuits of study; and the exercises which his daily tasks required, together with the company and conversation of these rational, well-informed, and thinking men, preserved his reason, and soon restored him to the full and free enjoyment of those faculties, from which both science and humanity afterward derived so many benefits.

The conduct of St. Francis, commonly called the holy Francis of Assisi, was in some degree similar; excepting that the madness of this fanatic continued throughout his life, while the delirium of Fothergill lasted but a day. This saint was born at Assisi, in the province of Umbria, in the year 1182. His real name of baptism was John; but, on account of the facility with which he acquired the French language, so necessary at that time in Italy, especially for the business for which he was intended, he was called Francis. He is said to have been born with the figure of a cross on his right shoulder, and to have dreamt that he was designed by heaven to promote the interests of that holy sign. His disposition was naturally mild, his comprehension quick, his feelings acute, his manners easy, his imagination vivid, and his passions inordinately warm. A careless and unrestrained indulgence of the propensities of youth had led him into a variety of vicious habits and libertine extravagances, until the solitude to which a fit of sickness confined him, brought him to a recollection, and forced him to reflect upon the dangerous tendency of his past misconduct. His mind started with horror at the dreadful scene his retrospection presented to his view; and he resolved to quit the company of his former associates, to reform the profligacy of his life, to restore his character, and to save, by penitence and prayer, his guilty soul. These serious reflections wrought so powerfully on his dejected mind, that he fell into an extravagant kind of devotion, more resembling madness than religion. Fixing on a passage in St. Matthew, in which our Saviour desires his apostles to *provide neither gold nor silver, nor brass in their purses; nor scrip for their journey; neither two coats, neither shoes, nor yet staves,* he was led to consider a voluntary and absolute poverty as the essence of the gospel, and to prescribe this poverty as a sacred rule, both to himself and to the few who followed him. He accordingly wandered through the streets of Assisi, in garments that scarcely concealed his nakedness, in order, as he said, to inure himself to the taunts and ridicule of his former companions, whom he now called the children of sin, and followers of satan. The father of the young saint, supposing, from these extravagances, that the sickness under which he had so long labored had disordered his intellects, prepared to provide him with some proper place of confinement, until time or medical regimen should restore him to his right senses; but the saint, having been informed of his father's friendly intention, declined his parental care, and quitting his house, sought a sanctuary in the palace of the bishop of Assisi. The diocesan immediately sent to the father of the fugitive, and, after hearing him upon the subject of his right to provide for the safety of his son, he turned calmly to the son and desired him to reply. The son immediately tore off the tattered garments which he then wore, and casting them with scorn and indignation at the feet of his astonished parent exclaimed, *"there, take back all your property. You were, indeed, my earthly father; but henceforth I disclaim you; for I own no father but him who is in heaven."* The bishop, either really or affectedly delighted with this unnatural rant of the young enthusiast, threw his own mantle over the saint, and exhorted him to persevere in his holy resolution, and to cherish with increasing ardor, the divine inspiration of his pious mind. The frantic youth, animated by the warm approbation of the bishop proceeded in his religious course, and abandoning the city, retired into the deepest gloom of an adjacent forest, to indulge the fervors of that false enthusiasm which had overpowered his brain. In this retreat a second vision confirmed him in his holy office; and being encouraged by pope Innocent III, and Honorius, he established, in the year 1209, the Order of Saint Francis. If this ridiculous enthusiast had corrected the extravagances of his overheated imagination, by a cool and temperate exercise of his reason, by studying, like the celebrated physician we have just mentioned, some liberal science, he might, with the talents he possessed, have become a really useful member of society. But these wild shoots, if suffered to grow to any height, cannot afterward be easily eradicated: and even Fothergill, if he had lived like Francis, in an age of superstitious delusion, and had been encouraged to believe the truth of his fanatic conceptions, his temporary frenzy might have continued through life; and his character, instead of being revered as a promoter of an useful science, have been held up by an ignorant multitude to the contempt and ridicule of posterity.

The vacancy of solitude, by leaving the mind to its own ideas, encourages to a great excess these wild and eccentric sallies of the imagination. He who has an opportunity to indulge, without interruption or restraint the delightful musings of an excursive fancy, will soon lose all relish for every other pleasure, and neglect every employment which tends to interrupt the gratification of such an enchanting though dangerous propensity. During the quietude of a sequestered life, imagination usurps the throne of reason, and all the feeble faculties of the mind obey her dictates, until her voice becomes despotic. If the high powers be exercised on the agreeable appearances of nature, and the various entertainments, poetry, painting, music, or any of the elegant arts, are capable of affording,

> ... Then the inexpressive strain
>
> Diffuses its enchantment; fancy dreams
>
> Of sacred fountains, and elysian groves,
>
> And vales of bliss; the intellectual Power
>
> Bends from his awful throne a wandering ear,
>
> And smiles; the passions, gently smoothed away,
>
> Sink to divine repose, and love and joy
>
> Alone are waking.

But if the mind, as in the solitude of monastic seclusion, fixes its attention on ascetic subjects, and fires the fancy with unnatural legends, the soul, instead of sinking to divine repose, feels a morbid melancholy and discontented torpor, which extinguishes all rational reflection, and engenders the most fantastic visions.

Men even of strong natural understandings, highly improved by education, have, in some instances, not been able to resist the fatal effects of intense application, and long continued solitude. The learned Molanus, having, during a course of many years, detached his mind from all objects of sense, neglected all seasonable and salutary devotion, and giving an uncontrolled license to his imagination fancied, in the latter part of his life, that he was a *barley corn*; and although he received his friends with great courtesy and politeness, and conversed upon subjects both of science and devotion with great ease and ingenuity, he could never afterward be persuaded to stir from home, lest, as he expressed his apprehension, he should be picked up in the street, and swallowed by a fowl.

The female mind is still more subject to these delusions of disordered fancy; for, as their feelings are more exquisite, their passions warmer, and their imaginations more active than those of the other sex, solitude, when carried to excess, affects them in a much greater degree. Their bosoms are much more susceptible to the injurious influence of seclusion, to the contagion of example, and to the dangers of illusion. This may, perhaps, in some degree, account for the similarity of disposition which prevails in cloisters, and other institutions which confine women entirely to the company of each other. The force of example and habit is, indeed, in such retreats, surprisingly powerful. A French medical writer, of great merit, and undoubted veracity, relates, that in a convent of nuns, where the sisterhood was unusually numerous, one of those secluded fair ones was seized with a strange impulse to mew like a cat; that several others of the nuns in a short time followed her example; and that at length this unaccountable propensity became general throughout the convent; the whole sisterhood joined, at stated periods, in the practice of mewing, and continued it for several hours. But of all the extraordinary fancies recorded of the sex, none can exceed that which Cardan relates to have happened in one of the convents of Germany, during the fifteenth century. One of the nuns, who had long been secluded from the sight of man, was seized with the strange propensity to bite all her companions; and extraordinary as it may seem, this disposition spread until the whole house was infected with the same fury. The account, indeed, states, that this mania extended even beyond the walls of the convent, and that the disease was conveyed to such a degree from cloister to cloister, throughout Germany, Holland, and Italy, that the practice at length prevailed in every female convent in Europe.

The instances of the pernicious influence of a total dereliction of society, may possibly appear to the understandings of the present generation extravagant and incredible; but they are certainly true; and many others of a similar nature might be adduced from the most authentic histories of the times. The species, when prevented from enjoying a free intercourse and rational society with each other, almost change their nature; and the mind, feeding continually on the melancholy musings of the imagination, in the cold and cheerless regions of solitude, engenders humors of the most eccentric cast. Excluded from those social communications which nature enjoins, with the means of gratifying the understanding, amusing the senses, or interesting the affections, fancy roves at large into unknown spheres, and endeavors to find in ideal forms entertainment and delight. Angelic visions, infernal phantoms, amazing prodigies, the delusions of alchemy, the frenzies of philosophy, and the madness of metaphysics, fill the disordered brain. The intellect fastens upon some absurd idea, and fosters it with the fondest affection, until its increasing magnitude subdues the remaining powers of sense and reason. The slightest retrospect into the conduct of the solitary professors of every religious system, proves the lamentable dangers to which they expose their mental faculties, by excluding themselves from the intercourse of rational society. From the prolific womb of solitude sprung all the mysterious ravings and senseless doctrines of the New Platonists. The same cause devoted the monks and anchorites of the Christian church to folly and fanaticism. Fakirs, Bramins, and every other tribe of religious enthusiasts, originated from the same source. By abandoning the pleasures of society, and renouncing the feelings of nature, they sacrificed reason upon the altar of superstition, and supplied its place with ecstatic fancies, and melancholy musings. There is nothing more evident, than that our holy religion, in its original constitution, was set so far apart from all refined speculations, that it seemed in a manner diametrically opposite to them. The great founder of Christianity gave one simple rule of life to all men; but his disciples, anxious to indulge the natural vanity of the human mind, and misled, in some degree, by the false philosophy which at that period overspread the heathen world, introduced various doctrines of salvation, and new schemes of faith. Bigotry, a species of superstition never known before, took place in men's affections, and armed them with new jealousies against each other: barbarous terms and idioms were every day invented; monstrous definitions imposed, and hostilities, the fiercest imaginable, exercised on each other by the contending parties. Fanaticism, with all the train of visions, prophecies, dreams, charms, miracles, and exorcises, succeeded; and spiritual feats, of the most absurd and ridiculous nature, were performed in monasteries, or up and down, by their mendicant or itinerant priests and ghostly missionaries. Solitude impressed the principles upon which these extravagances were founded, with uncommon force on the imagination; and the mind, working itself into holy fervors and inspirations, give birth to new extravagances. The causes which operated on the minds of men to produce such ridiculous effects, acted with double force on the ardent temper, warm imagination, and excessive sensibility of the female world. That which was mere fantasy with the one sex, became frenzy with the other. Women, indeed, are, according to the opinion of Plato, the nurses of fanaticism; and their favorite theme is that which has been dignified by the appellation of *a sublime passion for poetry*: an ardent, refined love of heaven; but which, in fact, is only the natural effects of the heart, swollen intumescently by an unreined, prolific, and too ardent imagination. Instances of this kind are discoverable in all the accounts that have been published of the holy fervors of these penitents, particularly in those of Catherine of Sienna, of Joan of Cambray, of Angelina of Foligny, of Matilda of Saxony, of Maria of the Incarnation, of Mary Magdalen of Pazzio, of Gertrude of Saxony, and many others. The celebrated Armelle, who was born in the year 1606, at Campenac, in the diocese of St. Malo, and who died at Vannes in the year 1671, possessed great personal beauty, a quick and lively mind, and an uncommon tenderness of heart. Her parents, who were honest and industrious villagers, placed her as a menial servant in the house of a neighboring gentleman, with whom she lived for five and thirty years in the practice of the most exemplary piety and extraordinary virtue, at least, according to the accounts which he gave from time to time of her conduct. During the time she resided with this gentleman, his groom, finding the kitchen door fastened, had the curiosity to peep through the key-hole, where he discovered the pious maid, in a paroxysm of divine ecstacy, performing the humble office of spitting a capon. The agitation of this holy spirit so affected the mind of the astonished youth, that, it is said by the Ursuline sister who has written the life of this great luminary of French sanctity, under the title of *The school for the love of God*, he became immediately enamored with the beauties of religion, and renouncing the pomps and vanities of the world, entered into a monastery, at the same time that his holy companion thought proper to withdraw from future observation into the convent of Vannes, where she devoted the remainder of her life, and died, as it is reported, in an excess of divine love. The youthful days of Armelle had been passed in almost total solitude; for her occupation at the house in which she was placed by her parents, was confined entirely to the kitchen, and she had scarcely any other intercourse than with its furniture. It appears, however, from the history of her life, that she was from her childhood excessively fond of reciting an *ave* or *paternoster*; and while occupied in tending the flocks, her original employment, amused herself in telling her rosary; "by which means," says the Ursuline sister, "she made, even in her pastoral state of simplicity and ignorance, such great advances in divine love that, the first moment she was allowed to pay her adoration to the crucifix the fervency of her pious passion burst forth with such ecstacy, that she eagerly snatched the holy object to her arms, and embraced it with a transport so warmly affectionate, that streams of tenderness rushed from her eyes."

It is truly said by a celebrated English writer, to be "of the utmost importance to guard against extremes of every kind in religion. We must beware lest by seeking to avoid one rock we split upon another. It has been long the subject of remark, that superstition and enthusiasm are two capital sources of delusion: superstition, on the one hand, attaching men with immoderate zeal to the ritual and external points of religion; and enthusiasm, on the other, directing their whole attention to internal emotions and mystical communications with the spiritual world; while neither the one nor the other had paid sufficient regard to the great moral duties of the Christian life. But running with intemperate eagerness from these two great abuses of religion, men have neglected to observe that there are extremes opposite to each of them, into which they are in hazard of precipitating themselves. Thus the horror of superstition has sometimes reached so far as to produce contempt for all external institutions; as if it were possible for religion to subsist in the world without forms of worship, or public acknowledgment of God. It has also happened, that some, who, in the main are well affected to the cause of goodness, observing that persons of a devout turn have at times been carried away by warm affections into unjustifiable excesses, have thence hastily concluded that all devotion was akin to enthusiasm; and separating religion totally from the heart and affections, have reduced it to a frigid observance of what they call the rules of virtue." These extremes are to be carefully avoided. True devotion is rational and well founded; and consists in the lively exercise of that affection which we owe to the Supreme Being, comprehending several emotions of the heart, which all terminate in the same great object.

These are among the evils which an irrational solitude is capable of producing upon an unrestrained and misdirected imagination; but I do not mean to contend indiscriminately, that solitude is generally to be considered as dangerous to the free indulgence of this delightful faculty of the mind. Solitude, well chosen, and rationally pursued, is so far from being either the open enemy, or the treacherous friend of a firm and fine imagination, that it ripens its earliest shoots, strengthens their growth, and contributes to the production of its richest and most valuable fruits. To him who has acquired the happy art of enjoying in solitude the charms of nature, and of indulging the powers of fancy without impairing the faculty of reason

> … Whate'er adorns
>
> The princely dome, the column, and the arch,
>
> The breathing marble, and the sculptured gold,
>
> Beyond the proud possessor's narrow claim,
>
> His happy breast enjoys. For him the spring
>
> Distils her dews, and from the silken gem
>
> Its lucid leaves unfolds: for him the hand
>
> Of autumn tinges every fertile branch

With blooming gold, and blushes like the morn.
Each passing hour sheds tribute from her wings;
And still new beauties meet his lonely walk,
And loves unfelt attract him. Not a breeze
Flies o'er the meadow; not a cloud imbibes
The setting sun's effulgence; not a strain
From all the tenants of the warbling shade
Ascends, but whence his bosom can partake
Fresh pleasure, unreproved. Nor thence partake
Fresh pleasure only: for the attentive mind,
By this harmonious action on her powers,
Becomes herself harmonious.

Chapter V
The effects of solitude on a melancholy mind

A disposition to enjoy the silence of sequestered solitude, and a glowing distaste of the noisy tumults of public life, are the earliest and most general symptoms of approaching melancholy. The heart, on which felicity was used to sit enthroned, becomes senseless to the touch of pleasure; the airy wing of high delight sinks prostrate to the earth on broken pinions: and care and anxiety, chagrin, and regret, load the mind with distempering ideas, and render it cheerless and forlorn. The dawning sun, and heaven lighted day, give no pleasure to the sickened senses of the unhappy sufferer. His only pleasure is to "commune with his own griefs;" and for this purpose he seeks some gloomy glen,

"Where bitter boding melancholy reigns

O'er heavy sighs and care disordered thoughts."

But a mind thus disposed, however it may for a time console its sorrows, by retiring from the world, thereby becomes more weak and helpless. Solitude in such cases, increases the disorder, while it softens its effects. To eradicate the seeds of this dreadful malady, the imagination should be impressed with some new, contrary, and more powerful bias than that which sways the mind, which can only be turned from its course of thought by shifting the object of its reflection, and giving entrance to new desires. A melancholy mind therefore, should be weaned by degrees from its disposition to solitude, should be agreeably interrupted in its musings, and be induced to relish the varying pleasures of the world. But, above all, those scenes and subjects which have any connexion, however remotely, with the cause of the complaint, must be cautiously avoided. The seeds of this dreadful malady are, in general, very deeply planted in the constitution of the patient, however accidental the circumstances may be when relieved from its oppression, is, if left to itself, always in danger of relapsing into its former habit. This circumstance alone is sufficient to show how unfriendly solitude must be to the cure of this complaint. If, indeed, the patient be so far gone as to leave no hope of recovery; if his desponding heart be incapable of any new impression; if his mind forgoes all custom of mirth; if he refuse to partake of any healthful exercise or agreeable recreation: and the soul sinks day after day into deeper dejection, and threatens nature with madness or with death, solitude is the only resource. When melancholy seizes, to a certain degree, the mind of an Englishman, it almost uniformly leads him to put a period to his existence; while the worst effect it produces on a Frenchman, is to induce him to turn Carthusian. Such dissimilar effects, proceeding from the operation of the same cause, in different persons, can only be accounted for from the greater opportunities which there is in France than in England to hide the sorrows of the mind from the inspection of the world. An English hypochondriac would, perhaps, seldom destroy himself, if there were in England any monastic institution to which he could fly from the eye of public observation.

The mind, in proportion as it loses its proper tone, and natural elasticity, decreases in its attachments to society, and wishes to recede from the world and its concerns. There is no disorder of the mind, among all the various causes by which it may be affected, that destroys its force and activity so entirely as melancholy. It unties, as it were, all the relations, both physical and moral, of which society, in its most perfect state, consists, and sets the soul free from all sense of obligation. The private link which unites the species is destroyed; all inclination to the common intercourse of life is lost; and the only remaining disposition is for solitude. It is for this reason that melancholy persons are continually advised to frequent the theatres, masquerades, operas, balls, and other places of public diversion; to amuse themselves at home with cards, dice, or other games; or to infuse from the eyes of female beauty new life into their drooping souls. Certain it is, that great advantages may be derived by detaching the mind from those objects by which it is tortured and consumed; but to run indiscriminately, and with injudicious eagerness, into the pursuit of pleasures, without any predisposition to enjoy them, may rather tend to augment than diminish the disease.

The eye of melancholy views every object on its darkest and most unfavorable side, and apprehends disastrous consequences from every occurrence. These gloomy perceptions, which increase as the feelings become more indolent, and the constitution more morbid, bring on habitual uneasiness and chagrin upon the mind, and render every injury, however small and trifling it may be, irksome and insupportable. A settled dejection ensues; and the miserable patient avoids every scene in which his musings may be liable to interruption; the few enjoyments he is yet capable of feeling in any degree impeded; or which may call upon him to make the slightest exertion; and by withdrawing himself from society into solitude, neglects the exercises and recreations by which his disease might be relieved. Instead of endeavoring to enlighten the dark gloom which involves his mind, and subdues his soul, by regarding with a favorable eye all that gives a true value and high relish to men of sound minds and lively dispositions, he fondly follows the phantom which misleads him, and thereby sinks himself more deeply into the moody fanes of irremediable melancholy: and if the bright rays of life and happiness penetrate by chance into the obscurity of his retreat instead of feeling any satisfaction from the perception of cheerfulness and content, he quarrels with the possessor of them, and converts their enjoyments into subjects of grievance, in order to torment himself.

Unfavorable, however, as a dreary and disconsolate solitude certainly is to the recovery of a mind labouring under this grievous affliction, it is far preferable to the society of licentious companions, and to wild scenes of inebriating dissipation. Worldly pleasures, and sensual gratifications of every description, when intemperately pursued, only drive a melancholy mind into a more abject state of dejection. It is from rational recreation, and temperate pleasures alone, that an afflicted mind can receive amusement and delight. The only scenes by which the mudded current of his mind can be cleared, or his stagnated system of pleasure refreshed, must be calm, cheerful, and temperate, not gay. Melancholy is of a sedate and pensive character, and flies from whatever is hurrying and tumultuous. How frequently do men of contemplative dispositions conceive a distaste for the world, only because they have unthinkingly engaged so ardently in the pursuits of pleasure, or of business, that they have been prevented for a length of time, from collecting their scattered ideas, and indulging their natural habits of reflection! But in striving to reclaim a melancholy mind, it is necessary to attend to the feelings of the heart, as well as the peculiar temper of the mind. A gloomy, disturbed, unquiet mind, is highly irritated, and its disease of course increased, by the company and conversation of those whose senseless bosoms are incapable of feeling the griefs it endures, or the complaints it utters. This, indeed, is another cause which drives melancholy persons from society into solitude; for how few are there whose tenderness leads them to sympathize with a brother in distress, or to contribute a kind aid to eradicate the thorns which rankle in his heart! Robust characters, in whose bosoms nature has planted the impenetrable shield of unvarying health, as well as those whose minds are engrossed by the charms of uninterrupted prosperity, can form no idea of the secret but severe agonies which shake the system of valetudinary men: nor feel any compassion for the tortures which accompany a wounded and afflicted spirit, until the convulsive frame proclaims the dreadful malady, or increasing melancholy sacrifices its victim on the altar of self-destruction. The gay associates of the unfeeling world view a companion suffering under the worst of nature's evils, with cold indifference, or affected concern; or, in the career of pleasure, overlook the miseries he feels until they hear that exhausted wo has induced him to brave the anger of the Almighty, and to rush from mortal misery, uncalled, into the awful presence of his Creator. Dreadful state! The secrecy and silence, indeed, with which persons of this description conceal the pangs that torture their minds, is among the most dangerous symptoms of the disease. It is not, indeed, easy to hide from the anxious and attentive eye of real friendship the feelings of the heart; but to the careless and indifferent multitude of common acquaintances, the countenance may wear the appearance not only of composure, but even of gayety, while the soul is inwardly suffering the keenest anguish of unutterable wo. The celebrated Carlini, a French actor of great merit, and in high reputation with the public, for the life, whim, frolic, and vivacity with which he nightly entertained the Parisian audiences, applied to a physician to whom he was not personally known, for advice, and represented to him that he was subject to attacks of the deepest melancholy. The physician advised him to amuse his mind by scenes of pleasure, and particularly directed him to frequent the Italian Comedy; "for," continued he, "your distemper must be rooted, indeed, if the acting of the lively Carlini does not remove it." "Alas!" exclaimed the unhappy patient, "I am the very Carlini whom you recommend me to see; and while I am capable of filling Paris with mirth and laughter, I am myself the dejected victim of melancholy and chagrin."

Painful as it may be to a person who is laboring under the oppression of melancholy, to associate with those who are incapable of sympathizing with his feelings, or who neglect to compassionate his sufferings, yet he should not fly from the presence of men into solitude; for solitude will unavoidably aggravate and augment his distress inasmuch as it tends to encourage that musing and soliloquy to which melancholy is invariably prone. It is the most dangerous resource to which he can fly; for, while it seems to promise the fairest hope of relief, it betrays the confidence reposed in it; and instead of shielding its votary from that conflict which disturbs his repose, it renders him defenceless, and delivers him unarmed to his bitterest enemy.

The boldest spirits and firmest nerves cannot withstand the inroads of melancholy merely by their own strength. It damps the courage of the most enterprising mind, and makes him who was before upon all occasions, fearless and unawed, shrink even from the presence of his fellow creatures. Company of every description becomes displeasing to him; he dreads the idea of visiting; and if he is induced to quit the domestic solitude into which he retires, it is only when the glorious, but to him offensive, light of heaven is concealed in congenial darkness; and the shades of night hide him from the observation of man. An invitation to social entertainment alarms his mind; the visit even of a friend becomes painful to his feelings; and he detests every thing which lightens the gloom in which he wishes to live, or which tends to disturb his privacy, or remove him from his retreat.

Rousseau, toward the latter part of his life, abandoned all intercourse with society under a notion, which was the effect of his melancholy disposition, that the world had conceived an unconquerable antipathy against him; and that his former friends, particularly Hume, and some philosophers in France, not only had entered into confederacy to destroy his glory and repose, but to take away his life. On departing from England, he passed through Amiens, where he met with Gresset, who interrogated him about his misfortunes, and the controversies in which he had been engaged; but Rousseau only answered, "You have got the art of making a parrot speak, but you are not yet possessed of the secret of giving language to a bear:" and when the magistrates of the city wished to confer on him some marks of their esteem, he refused all their offers, and considered these flattering civilities like the insults which were lavished in the same form on the celebrated Sancho in the island of Barataria. To such extent, indeed, did his disordered imagination carry him, that he thought one part of the people looked upon him like Lazarillo de Tormes, who being fixed to the bottom of a tub, with only his head out of water, was carried from one town to another to amuse the vulgar. His bad health, a strong and melancholy imagination, a too nice sensibility, a jealous disposition, joined with philosophic vanity, and his uncommon devotion to solitude, tended to prepossess him with those wrong and whimsical ideas. But it must be confessed that the opposition he met with from different ranks of persons, at several periods of his life, was extremely severe. He was driven at one time from France, in which he had before been distinguished by his writings, and highly honored. At another time he was chased from Geneva, the place of his nativity, and of his warmest affection. He was exiled from Berne with disgrace; expelled, with some appearance of injustice, from Neufchatel; and even banished from his tranquil solitude on the borders of the lake of Bienne. His disposition therefore to avoid society, must not be entirely attributed to his melancholy disposition; nor his love of solitude to a misanthropic mind. Every acute and scientific observer of the life and character of this extraordinary man will immediately perceive that the seeds of that melancholy disposition, and fretful temper, which through life destroyed his repose, were sown by nature in his constitution. He confesses indeed, to use his own words, that "a proud misanthropy, and peculiar contempt for the riches and pleasures of the world, constituted the chief traits of his character." This proud spirit and contemptuous mind were mixed with an extreme sensibility of heart, and an excessive indolence of disposition; and his body, which was naturally feeble, suffered, from ill health, the keenest agonies, and most excruciating disorders, to which the human frame is incident. Persecution also had levelled the most pointed and severely barbed shafts against him; and he was forced to endure, amidst the pangs of poverty, and the sorrows of sickness, all that envy, hatred, and malice, could inflict. It has been said, that the persecutions he experienced were not so much excited by the new dogmas, or eccentric paradoxes, which, both on politics and religion, pervade all his writings, as by the refinement of his extraordinary talents, the wonderful splendor of his eloquence, and the increasing extent of his fame. His adversaries certainly pursued him, not only with bigotry and intolerance, but with an inconsistency which revealed, in a great degree, the secret motives by which they were actuated; for they condemned, with the sharpest virulence, the freedom of his religious tenets, even in places where the religious creed of Voltaire was held in the highest admiration, and where atheism had collected the most learned advocates, and displayed the very standard of infidelity and disbelief. Harassed by the frowns of fortune, and pursued with unrelenting enmity by men whose sympathy and kindness he had anxiously endeavored to obtain, it is scarcely surprising that the cheerfulness of his disposition, and the kindness of his heart, should be subdued by those sentiments of aversion and antipathy which he fancied most of his intimates entertained against him: and the invectives from the pen of his former friend and confidant, Voltaire, together with many others that might be adduced, particularly the letter which was fabricated in the name of the king of Prussia, for the purpose of exposing him to ridicule, prove that his suspicions on the subject were not unfounded. The voice, indeed of mankind, seems ready to exclaim that this eccentric philosopher was not only a misanthrope, but a madman; but those who are charitably disposed, will recollect that he was a martyr to ill health; that nature had bestowed upon him a discontented mind; that his nerves were in a continued state of irritation; and that to preserve equanimity of temper when goaded by the shafts of calumny and malice, requires such an extraordinary degree of fortitude and passive courage as few individuals are found to possess. His faults are remembered, while the wonderful bloom and uncommon vigor of his genius, are forgotten or concealed. The production from which his merits are in general estimated, is that which is called "The Confessions:" a work written under the pressure of calamity, in sickness and in sorrow; amidst fears, distresses, and sufferings; when the infirmities which accompany old age, and the debility which attends continued ill health, had injured the tone of his mind, overpowered his reason, and perverted his feelings to such a degree, as to create an almost total transformation of the character of the man, and deprive him of his identity: but this degrading work ought, in candor, to be considered as a deplorable instance of the weakness of human nature, and how unable it is to support its own dignity when attacked by the adversities of fortune, and the malice of mankind. The greatness of Rousseau ought to be erected on a different basis: for his earliest works are certainly sufficient to support the extent of his fame as an author, however they may, on particular subjects, expose his integrity as a man.

The anxieties which a vehemence of imagination, and a tender texture of the nervous system at all times produce, are highly injurious to the faculties of the mind; and, when accompanied by sickness or by sorrow, wear out the intellect in proportion to its vigor and activity. To use the popular metaphor upon this subject, "The sword becomes too sharp for the scabbard;" and the body and the mind are thereby exposed to mutual destruction.

Religious melancholy is, of all other descriptions of this dreadful disease, most heightened and aggravated by solitude. The dreadful idea of having irretrievably lost the divine favor, and of being an object unworthy of the intercession of our Saviour, incessantly haunts the mind, laboring under religious despondency; and the imagination being left, in solitude, entirely to its own workings, increases the horrors which such thoughts must unavoidably inspire.

> Her lash Tisiphone that moment shakes,
>
> The mind she scourges with a thousand snakes,
>
> And to her aid, with many a thundering yell;
>
> Calls her dire sisters from the gulf of hell!

These mutual tortures, even when heightened by the gloominess of solitude, are frequently still further increased by the mischievous doctrines of bigoted priests, who by mistaking the effects of nervous derangement, or theological errors, for the compunctious visitings of a guilty mind, establish and mature, by the injudicious application of scriptural texts, and precepts of casuistry, the very disease which they thus ignorantly and presumptuously endeavor to remove. The wound, thus tainted by the most virulent and corrosive of the intellectual poisons, becomes extremely difficult to cure. The pure and uncontaminated tenets of the Christian faith furnishes, perhaps, the surest antidotes; and when these balms of true comfort are infused by such enlightened and discerning minds as Luther, Tillotson, and Clark, the most rational hope may be entertained of a speedy recovery. The writings of those holy teachers confirm the truth of the observation, that the deleterious gloom of superstition assumes a darker aspect in the shades of retirement, and they uniformly exhort the unhappy victims of this religious error to avoid solitude as the most certain enemy of this dreadful infirmity.

Solitude, however, is not the only soil in which this noxious weed springs up, spreading around its baleful glooms; it sometimes appears with deeply rooted violence in minds unused to retirement of every kind. In the course of my practice as a physician, I was called upon to attend a young lady, whose natural disposition had been extremely cheerful, until a severe fit of sickness damped her spirits, and rendered her averse to all those lively pleasures which fascinate the youthful mind. The debility of her frame, and the change of her temper were not sufficiently attended to in the early stages of her convalescence. The anxiety of her mind was visible in the altered features of her face; and she was frequently heard to express a melancholy regret that she had consumed so many hours in the frivolous, though innocent, amusements of the age. Time increased, by almost imperceptible degrees, these symptoms of approaching melancholy; and at length exhibited themselves by penitential lamentations of the sin she had committed with respect to the most trifling actions of her life, and in which no shadow of offence could possibly be found. At the time I was called in, this superstitious melancholy was attended with certain indications of mental derangement. The distemper clearly originated in the indisposition of the body, and the gloomy apprehensions which disease and pain, had introduced into the mind, during a period of many months. This once lively, handsome, but now almost insane female, was daily attacked with such violent paroxysms of her complaint, that she lost all sense of her situation, and exclaimed, in horrid distraction and deep despair, that her perdition was already accomplished, and that *the fiends were waiting to receive her soul, and plunge it into the bitterest torments of hell.* Her constitution, however, still fortunately retained sufficient strength to enable me, by the power of medicine, gradually to change its temperament, and to reduce the violence of the fever which had been long preying upon her life. Her mind became more calm in proportion as her nerves recovered their former tone; and when her intellectual powers were in a condition to be acted on with effect, I successfully counteracted the baleful effects of superstition by the wholesome infusion of real religion, and restored by degrees, a lovely, young, and virtuous woman, to her family and herself.

Another instance of a similar nature occurred very recently, in which the patient experienced all those symptoms, which prognosticate the approach of religious melancholy, and the completion of whose sorrow and despondency would quickly have been effected, if good fortune had not deprived her of the advice of an ignorant and bigoted priest, to whom her friends, when I was called in, had resolved to apply. This young lady, whose mind remained pure and uncorrupted amidst all the luxuries and dissipations which usually accompany illustrious birth and elevated station, possessed by nature great tranquillity of disposition, and lived with quietude and content, far retired from the pleasures of the world. I had been long acquainted with her family, and entertained for them the warmest esteem. The dangerous condition of her health gave me great anxiety and concern; for whenever she was left one moment to herself, and even in company, whenever she closed her eyes, a thousand horrid spectres presented themselves to her disordered mind, and seemed ready to devour her from every corner of the apartment. I inquired whether these imaginary spectres made any impression upon the affections of her heart: but she answered in the negative, and described the horrors which she felt from the supposed fierceness of their eyes, and the threatening gesticulations of their bodies. I endeavored to compose her by assuring her that they were the creatures of fancy, the wild chimeras of a weakened brain; that her long course of ill health had affected her mind; and that when a proper course of medicine, dietic regimen, and gentle exercise, had restored her strength, these dreadful appearances would give way to the most delightful visions. The course I pursued succeeded in a short time beyond my most sanguinary expectations, and I raised her languid powers to health and happiness. But if she had confided the anxieties of her mind to her confessor, instead of her physician, the holy father would, in all probability, have ascribed her gloomy apprehensions to the machinations of the devil, and have used nothing but pure spiritual antidotes to destroy them, which would have increased the melancholy, and possibly have thrown her into the darkest abyss of madness and despair.

This grievous malady, indeed, is not the exclusive offspring of mistaken piety and religious zeal; for it frequently invades minds powerful by nature, improved by science, and assisted by rational society. Health, learning, conversation, highly advantageous as they unquestionably are to the powers both of the body and the mind, have, in particular instances, been found incapable of resisting the influence of intense speculation, an atrabilarius constitution, and a superstitious habit. I have already mentioned the thick cloud of melancholy which obscured the latter days of the great and justly celebrated Haller, which were passed under the oppression of a religious despondency, that robbed him not only of all enjoyment, but almost of life itself. During the long period of four years, immediately antecedent to his death, he lived (if such a state could be called existence) in continual misery; except, indeed, at those short intervals when the returning powers of his mind enabled him, by the employment of his pen, to experience a temporary relief. A long course of ill health had forced him into an excessive use of opium, and by taking gradually increased quantities of that inspissated juice, he kept himself continually fluctuating between a state of mind naturally elevated and deeply dejected; for the first effects of this powerful drug are like those of a strong stimulating cordial, but they are soon succeeded by universal langour, or irresistable propensity to sleep, attended with dreams of the most agitated and enthusiastic nature. I was myself an eyewitness of the dreary melancholy into which this great and good man was plunged about two years before the kind, but cold, and though friendly, yet unwelcome hand of death, released him from his pains. The society, which, during that time, he was most solicitous to obtain, was that of priests and ecclesiastics of every description: he was uneasy when they were not with him: nor was he always happy in his choice of these spiritual comforters; for though, at times, he was attended by some of the most enlightened and orthodox divines of the age and country in which he lived, he was at others surrounded by those whom nothing but the reduced and abject state of his faculties would have suffered him to endure. But during even this terrible subversion of his intellectual powers, his love of glory still survived in its original radiance, and defied all the terrors both of hell and earth to destroy or diminish their force. Haller had embraced very deep and serious notions of the importance of Christianity to the salvation of the soul, and the redemption of mankind, which, by the ardency of his temper, and the saturnine disposition of his mind, were carried into a mistaken zeal and apprehension; and, instead of affording the comfort and consolation its tenets and principles are so eminently calculated to inspire, aggravated his feelings and destroyed his repose. In a letter which he wrote a few days before his death, to his great and good friend, the celebrated Heyne, of Gottingen, in which he announces the deep sense he entertained from his great age and multiplied infirmities, of his impending dissolution, he expressed his firm belief of revelation, and his faith in the mercy of God, and the intercession of Jesus Christ; but hints his fears lest the manifold sins, and the various errors and transgressions which the natural frailty of man must have accumulated during a course of seventy years, should have rendered his soul too guilty to expect the promised mercy to repentant sinners, and earnestly requests of him to inquire of his acquaintance Less, the virtuous divine of that place, whether he could not furnish him with some pious work that might tend to decrease the terrors he felt from the idea of approaching death, and relieve his tortured spirit from the apprehension of eternal punishment. The sentiments which occupied the mind of this pious philosopher when the dreaded hour actually arrived, whether it was comforted by the bright rays of hope, or dismayed into total eclipse by the dark clouds of despair, those who surrounded his dying couch have not communicated to the world. Death, while it released both his body and his mind from the painful infirmities and delusions under which they had so long and so severely suffered, left his fame, which, while living, he had valued much dearer than his life, exposed to the cruel shafts of slander and malevolence. A young nobleman of the canton of Berne, either moved by his own malice, or made an instrument of the malice of others, asserted in a letter, which was for a long time publicly exhibited in the university of Gottingen, that Haller had in his last moments denied his belief of the truth of Christianity. But those by whom he was then surrounded, betray, by the propagation of this falsehood, the fears they entertain of the firm support which his approbation would have given to that pure and pious system of religion, which they, it is well known, are so disposed to destroy. For certain it is, that Haller never doubted any of the attributes of the Deity, except his mercy; and this doubt was not the offspring of infidelity, but a crude abortion of that morbid melancholy which, during his latter days, settled so severely on his distempered mind. The same dread which he entertained of death, has been felt with equal if not greater horror, by minds as powerful and less superstitious. He candidly confessed the important and abstruse point upon which he had not been able to satisfy himself. His high sense of virtue made even his own almost exemplary and unblemished life appear, in his too refined speculations, grossly vicious. Mercy, he knew, must unavoidably, be correlative with justice; and he unfortunately conceived that no repentance, however sincere, could so purify the sinful, and, as he imagined, deplorable corruption of his soul, as to render it worthy of divine grace. So utterly had the melancholy dejection of his mind deprived him of a just sense of his character, and perfect knowledge of the nature of the Almighty. The mournful propensity of this great man must, if he had passed his days either in pious abstinence, or irrational solitude, have hurried him rapidly into irrecoverable frenzy; but Haller enjoyed the patronage of the great, the conversation of the learned, the company of the polite; and he not only suspended the effects of his malady, and of the medicines by which he attempted to relieve it, by these advantages, but by the sciences, which he so dearly loved and so successfully cultivated. The horrible evil, however, bowed him down in spite of all his efforts, and particularly oppressed him whenever he relaxed from his literary pursuits, or consulted his ghostly comforters on the lost condition of his soul.

Solitude, to a mind laboring under these erroneous notions of religion, operates like a rack, by which the imagination inflicts the severest tortures on the soul. A native of Geneva, a young man of very elegant manners, and a highly cultivated mind, some time since consulted me upon the subject of a nervous complaint, which I immediately discovered to be the consequence of a mistaken zeal for religion, a disposition naturally sedentary, and a habit which is too frequently indulged in solitude by unthinking youth. These circumstances had already made the most dreadful inroads both on his body and his mind. His emaciated frame was daily enfeebled by his paralyzed intellects, and he at length fell into a settled melancholy, which continued four years to defy the power of medicine, and finally destroyed his nervous system. A strong conviction of the heinous sin into which the blindness of his passion and evil example, had led him, at length flashed suddenly on his mind, and he felt, with the keenest compunctions of a wounded conscience, how impious he must appear to the all-seeing eye of the great Creator. Consternation and dismay seized his guilty mind; and the sense of virtue and religion, which he was naturally disposed to entertain, served only to increase his horror and distraction. He would have sought a refuge from the arrows of remorse under the protecting shields of penitence and prayer, but a scrupulous apprehension interposed the idea that it would be profanation in so guilty a sinner to exercise the offices of a pure and holy religion. He at length, however, proceeded to confession; but recollecting, after every disclosure, that he had still omitted many of his transgressions, additional horror seized upon his mind and tortured his feelings on the irrecoverable condition of his guilty soul. At intervals, indeed, he was able to perceive that the perturbations of his mind were the produce of his disorganized frame and disordered spirit; and he endeavored to recruit the one by air and exercise, and to dissipate the other by scenes of festivity and mirth: but his disorder had fixed his fibres too deeply in his constitution to be eradicated by such slight and temporary remedies. From the inefficacious antidotes of social pleasure and worldly dissipation, he was induced to try the calm and sedentary effects of solitary study; but his faculties were incapable of tasting the refined and elegant occupations of learning and the muse; his powers of reasoning were destroyed; his sensibilities, excepting on the subject of his complaint, were dried up; and neither the sober investigations of science, nor the more lively charms of poetry, were capable of affording him the least consolation. Into so abject a state, indeed, did his intellectual faculties at length fall, that he had not, during one period, sufficient ability to compute the change due to him from any piece of coin in the common transactions of life; and he confessed that he had been frequently tempted, by the deepness of his distress, to release both his body and his mind from their cruel sufferings, and "to shake impatiently his great affliction off" by self destruction; but the idea of heaping new punishment on his soul, by the perpetration of this additional crime, continually interposed, and saved him from the guilty deed. During this state of mental derangement, he fortunately met with a liberal minded and rational divine, who, free from the errors of priestcraft, and possessed of a profound knowledge of the virtues of religion and the structure of the human mind, undertook the arduous but humane and truly philosophic task, of endeavoring to bring back his mind to a rational sense of its guilt, and to a firm hope of pardon through the intercession of our Saviour. Religion, that sweet and certain comforter of human woes, at length effected a partial recovery, and restored him to a degree of tranquillity and repose; but he still continued to suffer, for years afterward, so great a misery from the shattered condition of his nerves, that he could not even compose a letter upon the most trifling and indifferent subject without the greatest labor and pain. As his feelings had never been hurt by any sense of injury received from mankind, he entertained no antipathy to his species; but as he was conscious that his reduced state of health prevented him from keeping up any rational or pleasing intercourse with them, he felt a sort of abhorrence to society, and refused, even when advised by his physicians and intimate friends, to mingle in its pleasures, or engage in its concerns. The proposal, indeed, appeared as extravagant and absurd to his feelings, as if a man, almost choking under the convulsion of a confirmed asthma, had been told that it was only necessary for him to breathe freely in order to acquire perfect ease. This deplorable state of health induced him to consult several Italian and English physicians; and being advised to try the effects of a sea voyage, he set sail for Riga, where he safely arrived; but, after a residence of six months, found himself unaltered, and precisely in the same dreadful condition in which he had set sail. On his return, I was called in to his assistance. There were at this period but very few of those gloomy and noxious vapors of superstition which had so tormented his mind, remaining; but his body, and particularly his nervous system, was still racked with agonizing pains. I had the good fortune to afford him great relief; and when at times his sufferings were suspended, and his spirits enlivened by pleasing conversation, he was certainly one of the most entertaining men, both as to the vivacity of his wit, the shrewdness of his observations, the powers of his reasoning, and the solidity of his judgment, that I had ever known.

These instances clearly evince how dangerous solitude may prove to minds predisposed, by accident or nature, to indulge a misdirected imagination, either upon the common subjects of life, or upon the more important and affecting topic of religion; but it must not be concluded from the observations I have already made, that a rational retirement from the vices, the vanities, and the vexations of the world, is equally unfriendly, under all circumstances, to a sickly mind. The cool and quiet repose which seclusion affords, is frequently the most advantageous remedy which can be adopted for the recovery of a disturbed imagination. It would indeed be the height of absurdity to recommend to a person suffering under a derangement of the nervous system, the diversions and dissipations of public life, when it is known, by sad experience, as well as by daily observation, that the least hurry disorders their frame, and the gentlest intercourse palpitates their hearts, and shakes their brains, almost to distraction. The healthy and robust can have no idea how violent the slightest touch vibrates through the trembling nerves of the dejected valetudinarian. The gay and healthy, therefore, seldom sympathize with the sorrowful and the sick. This, indeed, is one reason why those who, having lost the firm and vigorous tone of mind which is so essentially necessary in the intercourses of the world, generally abandon society, and seek in the softness of solitude a solace for their cares and anxieties; for there they frequently find a kind asylum, where the soul rests free from disturbance, and in time appeases the violence of its emotions: for "the foster nurse of nature is repose." Experience, alas! sad experience, has but too well qualified me to treat of this subject. In the fond expectation of being able to re-establish my nervous system, and to regain that health which I had broken down, and almost destroyed by intense application, I repaired to the Circle of Westphalia, in order to taste the waters of Pyrmont, and to divert the melancholy of my mind by the company which resorts to that celebrated spring: but, alas! I was unable to enjoy the lively scene; and I walked through multitudes of the great, the elegant, and the gay, in painful stupor, scarcely recognizing the features of my friends, and fearful of being noticed by those who knew me. The charms of wit, and the splendors of youthful beauty, were to me as unalluring as age and ugliness, when joined to the deformities of vice, and the fatiguing prate of senseless folly. During this miserable impotence of soul, and while I vainly sought a temporary relief of my own calamity, I was hourly assailed by a crowd of wretched souls, who implored me to afford them my professional aid, to alleviate those pains which time, alas! had fixed in their constitutions and which depended more on the management and reformation of their own minds, than on the powers of medicine to cure. For—

> I could not minister to a mind diseased,
>
> Pluck from the memory a rooted sorrow,
>
> Raze out the written troubles of the brain,
>
> And, with a sweet oblivious antidote,
>
> Cleanse the stuff'd bosom of that perilous stuff
>
> Which weighed upon the heart.

To avoid these painful importunities, I flew from the tasteless scenes with abrupt and angry violence; and confining myself to the solitude of my apartments, passed the lingering day in dreary dejection, musing on the melancholy group from which I had just escaped. But my home did not long afford me an asylum. I was on the ensuing day assailed by a host of hypochondriacs, attended by their respective advisers, who, while my own nervous malady was raging at its full height, stunned me with the various details of their imaginary woes, and excruciated me the whole day with their unfounded ails and tormenting lamentations. The friendly approach

of night at length relieved me from their importunities; but my spirits
had been exhausted, my feelings so vexed, my patience so tried, and the
sensibilities of my mind so aggravated, by the persecution I had endured,
that—

"Tir'd nature's sweet restorer, balmly sleep,"

fled from my eyes; and I lay restless upon my couch, alive only to my
miseries, in a state of anguish more insupportable than my bitterest enemies
would, I hope, have inflicted on me. About noon, on the ensuing day, while
I was endeavoring to procure on the sofa a short repose, the princess Orlow,
accompanied by two other very agreeable Russian ladies, whose company
and conversation it was both my pride and my pleasure frequently to enjoy,
suddenly entered my apartment, to inquire after my health, of the state of
which they had received an account only a few hours before; but such was
the petulance of temper into which my disordered mind had betrayed me,
that I immediately rose, and with uncivil vehemence, requested they would
not disturb me. The fair intruders instantly left the room. About an hour
afterward, and while I was reflecting on the impropriety of my conduct, the
prince himself honored me with a visit. He placed himself on a chair close by
the couch on which I lay, and, with that kind affection which belongs to his
character, inquired, with the tenderest and most sympathizing concern, into
the cause of my disorder. There was a charm in his kindness and attention
that softened, in some degree, the violence of my pains. He continued his
visit for some time; and when he was about to leave me, after premising that
I knew him too well to suspect that superstition had any influence in his
mind, said, "Let me advise you, whenever you find yourself in so waspish
and petulant a mood, as you must have been in when you turned the princess
and her companions out of the room, to endeavor to check the violence of
your temper; and I think you will find it an excellent expedient for this
purpose, if, while any friend is kindly inquiring after your health, however
averse you may be at the moment to such an inquiry, instead of driving him
so uncivilly away, you would employ yourself in a silent mental repetition
of the Lord's prayer: it might prove very salutary, and would certainly be
much more satisfactory to your mind." No advice could be better imagined
than this was to divert the emotions of impatience, by creating in the mind
new objects of attention, and turning the raging current of distempered
thought into a more pure and peaceful channel. Experience, indeed, has
enabled me to announce the efficacy and virtue of this expedient. I have
frequently, by the practice of it, defeated the fury of petulant passions, and
completely subdued many of those absurdities which vex and tease us in
the hours of grief and during the sorrows of sickness. Others also to whom
I have recommended it, have experienced from it similar effects. The prince,
"my guide, philosopher, and friend," a few weeks after he had given me
this wise and salutary advice, consulted me respecting the difficulty he

frequently labored under in suppressing the violence of those transports of affection which he bore toward his young and amiable consort, and which, in a previous conversation on philosophic subjects, I had seriously exhorted him to check, under a conviction, that a steady flame is more permanent and pure than a raging fire. He asked me with some concern what expedient I could recommend to him as most likely to control those emotions which happy lovers are so anxious to indulge. "My dear friend," I replied, "there is no expedient can surpass your own; and whenever the intemperance of passion is in danger of subverting the dictates of reason, repeat the Lord's prayer, and I have no doubt you will foil its fury."

When the mind is thus enabled to check and regulate the effects of the passions, and bring back the temper to its proper tone and rational basis, the serenity and calmness of solitude assists the achievement, and completes the victory. It is then so far from infusing into the mind the virulent passions we have before described, that it affords a soft and pleasing balm to the soul; and instead of being its greatest enemy, becomes its highest blessing and its warmest friend.

Solitude, indeed, as I have already observed, is far from betraying well-regulated minds either into the miseries of melancholy, or the danger of eccentricism. It raises a healthy and vigorous imagination to its noblest production, elevates it when dejected, calms it when disturbed, and restores it, when partially disordered, to its natural tone. It is as in every other matter, whether physical or moral, the abuse of solitude which renders it dangerous; like every powerful medicine, it is attended, when misapplied, with most mischievous consequences: but when properly administered, is pleasant in its taste, and highly salutary in its effects. He who knows how to enjoy it can

> ... truly tell
>
> To live in solitude is with truth to dwell;
>
> Where gay content with healthy temperance meets,
>
> And learning intermixes all its sweets;
>
> Where friendship, elegance, and arts unite
>
> To make the hours glide social, easy, bright:
>
> He tastes the converse of the purest mind:
>
> Though mild, yet manly: and though plain, refined;
>
> And through the moral world expatiates wide
>
> Truth as his end, and virtue as his guide.

Chapter VI
The influence of solitude on the passions

The passions lose in solitude a certain portion of that regulating weight by which in society they are guided and controlled; the counteracting effects produced by variety, the restraints imposed by the obligations of civility, and the checks which arise from the calls of humanity, occur much less frequently in retirement than amidst the multifarious transactions of a busy world. The desires and sensibilities of the heart having no real objects on which their vibrations can pendulate, are stimulated and increased by the powers of imagination. All the propensities of the soul, indeed, experience a degree of restlessness and vehemence greater than they ever feel while diverted by the pleasures, subdued by the surrounding distresses, and engaged by the business of active and social life.

The calm which seems to accompany the mind in its retreat is deceitful; the passions are secretly at work within the heart; the imagination is continually heaping fuel on the latent fire, and at length the laboring desire bursts forth, and glows with volcanic heat and fury. The temporary inactivity and inertness which retirement seems to impose, may check, but cannot subdue the energies of spirit. The high pride and lofty ideas of great and independent minds may be, for a while, lulled into repose; but the moment the feelings of such a character are awakened by indignity or outrage, its anger springs like an elastic body drawn from its centre, and pierces with vigorous severity the object that provoked it. The perils of solitude, indeed, always increase in proportion as the sensibilities, imaginations, and passions of its votaries are quick, excursive, and violent. The man may be the inmate of a cottage, but the same passions and inclinations still lodge within his heart: *his* mansion may be changed, but *their* residence is the same; and though they appear to be silent and undisturbed, they are secretly influencing all the propensities of his heart. Whatever be the cause of his retirement, whether it be a sense of undeserved misfortune, the ingratitude of supposed friends, the pangs of despised love, or the disappointment of ambition, memory prevents the wound from healing, and stings the soul with indignation and resentment. The image of departed pleasures haunts the mind, and robs it of its wished tranquillity. The ruling passion still subsists; it fixes itself more strongly on the fancy; moves with greater agitation; and becomes, in retirement, in proportion as it is inclined to vice or virtue, either a horrid and tormenting spectre, inflicting apprehension and dismay, or a delightful and supporting angel, irradiating the countenance with smiles of joy, and filling the heart with peace and gladness.

> Blest is the man, as far as earth can bless,
>
> Whose measur'd passions reach no wild excess;
>
> Who, urged by nature's voice, her gifts enjoys,
>
> Nor other means than nature's force employs.
>
> While warm with youth the sprightly current flows,
>
> Each vivid sense with vigorous rapture glows;
>
> And when he droops beneath the hand of age,
>
> No vicious habit stings with fruitless rage;
>
> Gradual his strength and gay sensations cease,
>
> While joys tumultuous sink in silent peace.

The extraordinary power which the passions assume, and the improper channel in which they are apt to flow in retired situations, is conspicuous from the greater acrimony with which they are in general tainted in small villages than in large towns. It is true, indeed, that they do not always explode in such situations with the open and daring violence which they exhibit in the metropolis; but lie buried as it were, and mouldering in the bosom with a more malignant flame. To those who only observe the listlessness and languor which distinguish the characters of those who reside in small provincial towns, the slow and uniform rotation of amusements which fills up the leisure of their lives; the confused wildness of their cares; the poor subterfuges to which they are continually resorting, in order to avoid the clouds of discontent that impend in angry darkness, over their heads; the lagging current of their drooping spirits; the miserable poverty of their intellectual powers; the eagerness with which they strive to raise a card party; the transports they enjoy on the prospect of any new diversion or occasional exhibition; the haste with which they run toward any sudden, unexpected noise that interrupts the deep silence of their situation; and the patient industry with which, from day to day, they watch each other's conduct, and circulate reports of every action of each other's lives, will scarcely imagine that any virulence of passion can disturb the bosoms of persons who live in so quiet and seemingly composed a state. But the unoccupied time and barren minds of such characters cause the faintest emotions, and most common desires, to act with all the violence of high and untamed passions. The lowest diversions, a cock fighting, or a pony race, make the bosom of a country 'squire beat with the highest rapture; while the inability to attend the monthly ball fills the minds of his wife and daughter with the keenest anguish. Circumstances, which scarcely make any impression on those who reside in the metropolis, plunge every description of residents in a country village into all the extravagances of joy, or the dejection of sorrow; from the peer to the peasant, from the duchess to the dairy maid, all is rapture and convulsion. Competition is carried on for the humble honors and petty interests of a sequestered town, or miserable hamlet, with as much heat and rancor, as it is for the highest dignities and greatest emoluments of the state. Upon many occasions, indeed, ambition, envy, revenge, and all the disorderly and malignant passions, are felt and exercised with a greater degree of violence and obstinacy amidst the little contentions of claybuilt cottages, than ever prevailed amidst the highest commotions of courts. Plutarch relates that when Cæsar, after his appointment to the government of Spain, came to a little town, as he was passing the Alps, his friends, by way of mirth, took occasion to say, "Can there here be any disputes for offices, any contentions for precedency, or such envy and ambition as we behold among the great in all the transactions of imperial Rome?" The idea betrayed their ignorance of human nature; while the celebrated reply of their great commander, that *he would rather be the first man in this little town, than the second even in the imperial city,* spoke the language, not of an individual, but of the species; and instructed them that there is no place, however insignificant, in which the same passions do not proportionately prevail. The humble competitors for village honors, however low and subordinate they may be, feel as great anxiety for pre-eminence, as much jealousy of rivals, and as violent envy against superiors, as agitate the bosoms of the most ambitious statesmen in contending for the highest prize of glory, of riches, or of power. The manner, perhaps, in which these inferior candidates exert their passions may be less artful, and the objects of them less noble, but they are certainly not less virulent. "Having," says Euphelia, who had quitted London, to enjoy the quietude and happiness of a rural village, "been driven by the mere necessity of escaping from absolute inactivity, to make myself more acquainted with the affairs and happiness of this place, I am now no longer a stranger to *rural conversation* and employments; but am far from discerning in them more innocence or wisdom than in the sentiments or conduct of those with whom I have passed more cheerful and more fashionable hours. It is common to reproach the tea table and the park, with giving opportunities and encouragement to scandal I cannot wholly clear them from the charge, but must, however, observe, in favor of the modish prattlers, that if not by principle, we are at least by accident, less guilty of defamation than the country ladies. For, having greater numbers to observe and censure, we are commonly content to charge them only with their own faults or follies, and seldom give way to malevolence, but such as arises from injury or affront, real or imaginary, offered to ourselves. But in those distant provinces, where the same families inhabit the same houses from age to age, they transmit and recount the faults of a whole succession. I have been informed how every estate in the neighborhood was originally got, and find, if I may credit the accounts given me, that there is not a single acre in the hands of the right owner. I have been told of intrigues between beaus and toasts, that have been now three centuries in their quiet graves; and am often entertained with traditional scandal on persons of whose names there would have been no remembrance, had they not committed somewhat that might disgrace their descendants. If once there happens a quarrel between the principal persons of two families, the malignity is continued without end; and it is common for old maids to fall out about some election in which their grandfathers were competitors. Thus malice and hatred descend here with an inheritance; and it is necessary to be well versed in history, that the various factions of the country may be understood. You cannot expect to be on good terms with families who are resolved to love nothing in common; and in selecting your intimates, you are, perhaps, to consider which party you most favor in the barons' wars."

Resentments and enmities burn with a much more furious flame among the thinly-scattered inhabitants of a petty village, than amidst the ever varying concourse of a great metropolis. The objects by which the passions are set on fire are hidden from our view by the tumults which prevail in a crowded city, and the bosom willingly loses the pains which such emotions excite when the causes which occasioned them are forgot: but in country villages, the thorns by which the feelings have been hurt are continually before our eyes, and preserve on every approach toward them, a remembrance of the injuries sustained. An extreme devout and highly religious lady, who resided in a retired hamlet in Swisserland, once told me, in a conversation on this subject, that she had completely suppressed all indignation against the envy, the hatred, and the malice of her surrounding neighbors; for that she found they were so deeply dyed in sin, that a rational remonstrance was lost upon them; and that the only vexation she felt from a sense of their wretchedness arose from the idea that her soul would at the last day be obliged to keep company with such incorrigible wretches.

The inhabitants of the country, indeed, both of the lower and middling classes, cannot be expected to possess characters of a very respectable kind, when we look at the conduct of those who set them the example. A country magistrate, who has certainly great opportunities of forming the manners and morals of the district over which he presides, is in general puffed up with high and extravagant conceptions of the superiority of his wisdom, and the extent of his power; and raising his idea of the greatness of his character in an inverse proportion to his notions of the insignificance and littleness of those around him, he sits enthroned with fancied pre-eminence, the disdainful tyrant, rather than the kind protector of his neighbors. Deprived of all liberal and instructive society, confined in their knowledge both of men and things, the slaves of prejudice and the pupils of folly; with contracted hearts and degraded faculties the inhabitants of a country village feel all the base and ignoble passions, sordid rapacity, mean envy, and insulting ostentation more forcibly than they are felt either in the enlarged society of the metropolis, or even in the confined circle of the monastery.

The social virtues, indeed, are almost totally excluded from cloisters, as well as from every other kind of solitary institution: for when the habits, interests, and pleasures of the species are pent up by any means within a narrow compass, mutual jealousies and exasperations must prevail; every trifling immunity, petty privilege, and paltry distinction, becomes an object of the most violent contention; and increasing animosities at length reach to such a degree of virulence, that the pious flock is converted into a herd of famished wolves, eager to worry and devour each other.

The laws of every convent strictly enjoin the holy sisterhood to live in Christian charity and sincere affection with each other. I have, however, when attending these fair recluses in my professional character, observed many of them with wrinkles, that seemed rather the effect of angry perturbation, than of peaceful age, with aspects formed rather by envy, hatred, malice, and all uncharitableness, than by mild benevolence and singleness of heart. But I should do injustice if I did not declare, that I have seen some few who were strangers to such unworthy passions; whose countenances were unindented by their effects: and whose beauty and comeliness still shone in their native lustre and simplicity. It was, indeed, painful to reflect upon the sufferings which these lovely innocents must endure, until the thoughts of their lost hopes, defeated happiness, and unmerited wrongs, should have changed the milky kindness of their virtuous dispositions into the gall-like bitterness of vexation and despair; until the brightness of their charming features should be darkened by the clouds of discontent, which their continued imprisonment would create; and until their cheerful and easy tempers should be perverted by the corrosions of those vindictive passions which the jealous furies, with whom they were immured, and to whom they formed so striking a contrast, must in time so cruelly inflict. These lovely mourners, on entering the walls of a convent, are obliged to submit to the tyranny of an envious superior, or the jealousy of the older inmates, whose angry passions arise in proportion as they perceive others less miserable than themselves; and retiring, at the stated periods, from their joint persecution, they find that the gloomy solitude to which they have flown, only tends to aggravate and widen the wound it was expected to cure. It is, indeed, almost impossible for any female, however amiable, to preserve in the joyless gloom of conventual solitude the cheering sympathies of nature. A retrospect of her past life most probably exhibits to her tortured fancy, superstition stinging with scorpion like severity her pious mind; love sacrificed on the altar of family pride; or fortune ruined by the avarice of a perfidious guardian; while the future presents to her view the dreary prospect of an eternal and melancholy separation from all the enjoyments of society, and a continual exposure to the petulance and ill humor of the dissatisfied sisterhood. What disposition, however mild and gentle by nature, can preserve itself amidst such confluent dangers? How is it possible to prevent the most amiable tenderness of heart, the most lively and sensible mind from becoming, under such circumstances, a prey to the bitterness of affliction and malevolence? Those who have had an opportunity to observe the operation of the passions on the habits, humors, and dispositions of recluse females, have perceived with horror the cruel and unrelenting fury with which they goad the soul, and with what an imperious and irresistible voice they command obedience to their inclination.

The passion of love, in particular, acts with much greater force upon the mind that endeavors to escape from its effects by retirement, than it does when it is either resisted or indulged.

Retirement, under such circumstances, is a childish expedient; it is expecting to achieve that, by means of a fearful flight, which it is frequently too much for the courage and the constancy of heroes to subdue. Retirement is the very nest and harbor of this powerful passion. How many abandon the gay and jovial circles of the world, renounce even the most calm and satisfactory delights of friendship, and quit, without a sigh, the most delicious and highest seasoned pleasures of society, to seek in retirement the superior joys of love! a passion in whose high and tender delights the insolence of power, the treachery of friendship, and the most vindictive malice, is immediately forgot. It is a passion, when pure, that can never experience the least decay; no course of time, no change of place, no alteration of circumstances, can erase or lessen the ideas of that bliss which it has once imprinted on the heart. Its characters are indelible. Solitude, in its most charming state, and surrounded by its amplest, powers, affords no resource against its anxieties, its jealous fears, its tender alarms, its soft sorrows, or its inspiringly tumultuous joys. The bosom that is once deeply wounded by the barbed dart of real love, seldom recovers its tranquillity, but enjoys, if happy, the highest of human delights; and if miserable, the deepest of human torments. But, although the love-sick shepherd fills the lonely vallies, and the verdant groves, with the softest sighs, or severest sorrows, and the cells of the monasteries and convents resound with heavy groans and deep-toned curses against the malignity of this passion, solitude may perhaps, for a while suspend, if it cannot extinguish its fury. Of the truth of this observation, the history of those unfortunate, but real lovers, Abelard and Eloisa, furnishes a memorable instance.

In the twelfth century, and while Louis the Gross filled the throne of France, was born in the retired village of Palais, in Brittany, the celebrated Peter Abelard. Nature had lavished the highest perfections both on his person and his mind: a liberal education improved to their utmost possible extent the gifts of nature; and he became in a few years the most learned, elegant, and polite gentleman of his age and country. Philosophy and divinity were his favorite studies: and lest the affairs of the world should prevent him from becoming a proficient in them, he surrendered his birthright to his younger brethren, and travelled to Paris, in order to cultivate his mind under that great professor, William des Champeaux. The eminence he attained as a professor, while it procured him the esteem of the rational and discerning, excited the envy of his rivals. But, beside his uncommon merit as a scholar, he possessed a greatness of soul which nothing could subdue. He looked upon riches and grandeur with contempt; and his only ambition was to render his name famous among learned men, and to acquire the reputation of the greatest doctor of his age. But when he had attained his seven and twentieth year of age, all his philosophy could not guard him against the shafts of love. Not far from the place where Abelard read his lectures, lived a canon of the church of Notre Dame, named Fulbert, whose niece, the celebrated Eloisa, had been educated under his own eye with the greatest care and attention. Her person was well proportioned, her features regular, her eyes sparkling, her lips vermilion and well formed, her complexion animated, her air fine, and her aspect sweet and agreeable. She possessed a surprising quickness of wit, an incredible memory, and a considerable share of learning, joined with great humility and tenderness of disposition: and all these accomplishments were attended with something so graceful and moving, that it was impossible for those who saw her not to love her. The eye of Abelard was charmed, and his whole soul intoxicated in the passion of love, the moment he beheld and conversed with this extraordinary woman; and he laid aside all other engagements to attend to his passion. He was deaf to the calls both reason and philosophy, and thought of nothing but her company and conversation. An opportunity, fortunate for his love, but fatal to his happiness, soon occurred. Fulbert, whose affection for his niece was unbounded, willing to improve to the highest degree the excellency of those talents which nature had so bountifully bestowed on her, engaged

Abelard as her preceptor, and received him in that character into his house. A mutual passion strongly infused itself into the hearts of both pupil and preceptor. She consented to become his mistress, but, for a long time, refused to become his wife. The secret of their loves could not remain long concealed from the eyes of Fulbert, and the lover was dismissed from his house: but Eloisa flew with rapture to his arms, and was placed under the protection of his sister, where she remained; until, from the cruel vengeance which her uncle exercised on the unfortunate Abelard, she was induced at his request to enter into the convent of Argenteuil, and he into the monastery of St. Gildas. In this cloister, the base of which was washed by the waves of a sea less turbulent than the passions which disturbed his soul, the unfortunate Abelard, endeavored by the exercises of religion and study, to obliterate all remembrance of his love; but his virtue was too feeble for the great attempt. A course of many years, however, had passed in penitence and mortification, without any communication between them, and further time might possibly have calmed in a still greater degree the violence of their feelings; but a letter which Abelard wrote to his friend Philintus, in order to comfort him under some affliction which had befallen him, in which he related his affection for Eloisa with great tenderness, fell into her hands, and induced her to break through the silence which had so long prevailed, by writing to him a letter, the contents of which revived in his mind all the former furies of his passion. Time, absence, solitude, and prayer, had in no degree diminished the amiable tenderness of the still lovely Eloisa, or augmented the fortitude of the unfortunate Abelard. The composing influence of religion seems to have made an earlier impression upon his feelings than it did upon those of Eloisa; but he continually counteracted its effects, by comparing his former felicity with his present torments; and he answered Eloisa's letter, not as a moral preceptor, or holy confessor, but as a still fond and adoring lover; as a man whose wounded feelings were in some degree alleviated by a recollection of his former joys; and who could only console the sorrows of his mistress, by avowing an equal tenderness, and confessing the anguish with which their separation rent his soul. The walls of Paraclete resounded his sighs less frequently, and re-echoed less fervently with his sorrows, than those of St. Gildas; for his continued solitude, so far from affording him relief, had administered an aggravating medicine to his disease; and afforded that vulture, grief, greater leisure to tear and prey upon his disordered heart. "Religion," says he, "commands me to pursue virtue since I have nothing to hope for from love; but love still asserts its dominion in my fancy, and entertains itself with past pleasures; memory supplies the place of a mistress. Piety and duty are not always the fruits of retirement. Even in deserts, when the dew of heaven falls not on us, we love what we ought no longer to love. The passions, stirred up by solitude, fill those regions of death and silence; and it is very seldom that what ought to be is truly followed there, and that God only is loved and served."

The letters of Eloisa were soft, gentle, and endearing; but they breathed the warmest language of tenderness and unconquerable passion. "I have your picture," says she, "in my room. I never pass by it without stopping to look at it; and yet when you were present with me, I scarce even cast my eyes upon it. If a picture, which is but a mute representation of an object, can give such pleasure, what cannot letters inspire? Letters have souls; they have in them all that force which expresses the transports of the heart: they have all the fire of our passions; they can raise them as much as if the persons themselves were present; they have all the softness and delicacy of speech, and sometimes a boldness of expression even beyond it. We may write to each other; so innocent a pleasure is not forbidden us. Let us not lose, through negligence, the only happiness which is left to us, and the only one perhaps, which the malice of our enemies can never ravish from us. I shall read that you are my husband, and you shall see me address you as a wife. In spite of all your misfortunes, you may be what you please in your letters. Letters were first invented for comforting such solitary wretches as myself. Having lost the pleasure of seeing you, I shall compensate this loss by the satisfaction I shall find in your writings: there I shall read your most secret thoughts: I shall carry them always about me; I shall kiss them every moment. If you can be capable of jealousy, let it be for the fond curiosity I shall bestow on your letters, and envy only the happiness of those rivals. That writing may be no trouble to you, write always to me carelessly and without study: I had rather read the dictates of the heart than of the brain. I cannot live, if you do not tell me you always love me. You cannot but remember, (for what do not lovers remember?) with what pleasure I have passed whole days in hearing you discourse; how, when you was absent, I shut myself up from every one to write to you; how uneasy I was till my letter had come to your hands; what artful management was required to engage confidants. This detail, perhaps, surprises you, and you are in pain for what will follow: but I am no longer ashamed that my passion has had no bounds for you; for I have done more than all this: I have hated myself that I might love you. I came hither to ruin myself in a perpetual imprisonment, that I might make you live quiet and easy. Nothing but virtue, joined to a love perfectly disengaged from the commerce of the senses, could have produced such effects. Vice never inspires any thing like this. How did I deceive myself with the hopes that you would be wholly mine when I took the veil, and engaged myself to live for ever under your laws! For, in being professed, I vowed no more than to be yours only; and I obliged myself voluntarily to a confinement in which you denied to place me. Death only can make me leave the place where you have fixed me; and then too my ashes shall rest here, and wait for yours, in order to show my obedience and devotedness to you to the latest moment possible."

Abelard, while he strove, in his reply, to adhere to the dictates of reason, betrayed the lurking tenderness of his heart. "Deliver yourself, Eloisa," says he, "from the shameful remains of a passion which has taken too deep root. Remember that the least thought for any other than God is an adultery. If you could see me here, pale, meagre, melancholy, surrounded by a band of persecuting monks, who feel my reputation for learning as a reproach of their stupidity and ignorance, my emaciated figure as a slander on their gross and sensual corpulency, and my prayers as an example for their reformation, what would you say to the unmanly sighs, and unavailing tears, by which they are deceived? Alas! I am bowed down by the oppressive weight of love, rather than contrition for past offences. Oh, my Eloisa, pity me, and endeavor to free my laboring soul from its captivity! If your vocation be, as you say, my wish, deprive me not of the merit of it by your continual inquietudes: tell me that you will honor the habit which covers you by an inward retirement. Fear God that you may be delivered from your frailties. Love him, if you would advance in virtue. Be not uneasy in the cloister, for it is the dwelling of saints; embrace your bands, they are the chains of Jesus, and he will lighten them, and bear with you, if you bear them with humility and repentance. Consider me no more, I entreat you, as a founder, or as a person in any way deserving your esteem; for your encomiums do but ill agree with the multiplying weakness of my heart. I am a miserable sinner, prostrate before my Judge; and when the rays of grace break on my troubled soul, I press the earth with my lips, and mingle my sighs and tears in the dust. Couldest thou survey thy wretched lover thus lost and forlorn, thou wouldest no longer solicit his affection. The tenderness of thy heart would not permit thee to interpose an earthly passion, which can only tend to deprive him of all hopes of heavenly grace and future comfort. Thou wouldest not wish to be the object of sighs and tears, which ought to be directed to God alone. Canst thou, my Eloisa, become the confederate of my evil genius, and be the instrument to promote sin's yet unfinished conquest? What, alas! couldest thou not achieve with a heart, the weaknesses of which you so well know? But, oh! let me conjure you, by all the sacred ties, to forget for ever the wretched Abelard, and thereby contribute to his salvation. Let me entreat you by our former joys, and by our now common misfortunes, not to abet my destruction. The highest affection you can now show me, is to hide your tenderness from my view and to renounce me for ever. Oh,

Eloisa! be devoted to God alone; for I here release you from all engagements to me."

The conflict between love and religion tore the soul of Eloisa with pangs far more violent and destructive. There is scarcely a line of her reply to Abelard, that does not show the dangerous influence which solitude had given to the concealed, but unsmothered, passion that glowed within her breast. "Veiled as I am," she exclaims, "behold in what a disorder you have plunged me! How difficult it is to fight always for duty against inclination! I know the obligation which this sacred veil has imposed on me; but feel more strongly the power which a long and habitual passion has gained over my heart. I am the victim of almighty love: my passion troubles my mind, and disorders my senses. My soul is sometimes influenced by the sentiments of piety which my reflections inspire, but the next moment I yield myself up to the tenderness of my feelings, and to the suggestions of my affection. My imagination riots with wild excursion in the scenes of past delights. I disclose to you one moment what I would not have told you a moment before. I resolve no longer to love you; I consider the solemnity of the vow I have made, and the awfulness of the veil I have taken; but there arises, unexpectedly, from the bottom of my heart, a passion which triumphs over all these notions, and, while it darkens my reason, destroys my devotion. You reign in all the close and inward retreats of my soul; and I know not how nor where to attack you with any prospect of success. When I endeavor to break the chains which bind me so closely to you, I only deceive myself, and all my efforts serve only to confirm my captivity, and to rivet our hearts more firmly to each other. Oh! for pity's sake, comply with my request; and endeavor by this means, to make me renounce my desires, by showing me the obligation I am under to renounce you. If you are still a lover, or a father, oh! help a mistress, and give comfort to the distraction of an afflicted child. Surely these dear and tender names will excite the emotion either of pity or of love. Gratify my request; only continue to write to me, and I shall continue to perform the hard duties of my station without profaning that character which my love for you induced me to assume. Under your advice and admonition I shall willingly humble myself, and submit with penitence and resignation to the wonderful providence of God, who does all things for our sanctification; who, by his grace purifies all that is vicious and corrupt in our natures; and, by the inconceivable riches of his mercy, draws us to himself against our wishes, and by degrees opens our eyes to discern the greatness of that bounty which at first we are incapable of understanding. Virtue is too amiable not to be embraced when you reveal her charms, and vice too hideous not to be avoided when you show her deformities. When you are pleased, every thing seems lovely to me. Nothing is frightful or difficult when you are by. I am only weak when I am alone, and unsupported by you; and therefore it depends on you alone that I may be such as you desire. Oh! that you had not so powerful an influence over all my soul! It is your fears, surely, that make you thus deaf to my entreaties, and negligent of my desires: but what is there for you to fear? When we lived happily together you might have doubted whether it was pleasure or affection that united me to you; but the place from which I now indite my lamentations must have removed that idea, if it ever could find a place in your mind. Even within these gloomy walls, my heart springs toward you with more affection than it felt, if possible, in the gay and glittering world. Had pleasure been my guide, the world would have been the theatre of my joys. Two and twenty years only of my life had worn away, when the lover on whom my soul doated was cruelly torn from my arms; and at that age female charms are not generally despised; but, instead of seeking to indulge the pleasures of youth, your Eloisa, when deprived of thee, renounced the world, suppressed the emotions of sense, at a time when the pulses beat with the warmest ardor, and buried herself within the cold and cheerless region of the cloister. To you she consecrated the flower of her charms; to you she now devotes the poor remains of faded beauty; and dedicates to heaven and to you, her tedious days and widowed nights in solitude and sorrow."

The passion, alas! which Eloisa thus fondly nourished in her bosom, like an adder, to goad and sting her peace of mind, was very little of a spiritual nature; and the walls of Paraclete only re-echoed more fervent sighs than she had before breathed, and witnessed a more abundant flow of tears than she had shed in the cells of Argenteuil, over the memory of departed joys with her beloved Abelard. Her letters, indeed, show with what toilsome but ineffectual anxiety she endeavored to chasten her mind, and support her fainting virtue, as well by her own reasoning and reflection, as by his counsels and exhortations; but the passion had tenaciously rooted itself at the very bottom of her heart; and it was not until the close of life that she was able to repress the transports of her imagination, and subdue the wild sallies of her fond and fertile fancy. Personally separated from each other, she indulged a notion that her love could not be otherwise than pure and spiritual; but there are many parts of letters which show how much she was deceived by this idea; for in all the fancied chastity of their tender and too ardent loves,

> "Back thro' the pleasing maze of sense she ran,
>
> And felt within the slave of love and man."

The wild and extravagant excesses to which the fancy and the feelings of Eloisa were carried, was not occasioned merely by the warm impulses of unchecked nature; but were forced, to the injury of virtue, and the distraction of reason, by the rank hot bed of monastic solitude. The story of these celebrated lovers, when calmly examined, and properly understood, proves how dangerous it is to recede entirely from the pleasures and occupations of social life, and how deeply the imagination may be corrupted, and the passions inflamed, during a splenetic and ill-prepared retirement from the world. The frenzies which follow disappointed love, are of all others the most likely to settle into habits of the deepest melancholy. The finest sensibilities of the heart, the purest tenderness of the soul, when joined with a warm constitution, and an ardent imagination, experience from interruption and control the highest possible state of exasperation. Solitude confirms the feelings such a situation creates; and the passions and inclinations of a person laboring under such impressions are more likely to be corrupted and inflamed by the leisure of retirement, than they would be even by engaging in all the lazy opulence and wanton plenty of a debauched metropolis.

The affection which Petrarch entertained for Laura was refined, elevated, and virtuous, and differed, in almost every ingredient of it, from the luxurious fondness of the unfortunate Eloisa; but circumstances separated him from the beloved object; and he labored during many years of his life, under the oppression of that grievous melancholy which disappointment uniformly inflicts. He first beheld her as she was going to the church of the monastery of St. Claire. She was dressed in green, and her gown was embroidered with violets. Her face, her air, her gait, appeared something more than mortal. Her person was delicate, her eyes tender and sparkling, and her eyebrows black as ebony. Golden locks waved over her shoulders whiter than snow, and the ringlets were woven by the fingers of love. Her neck was well formed, and her complexion animated by the tints of nature, which art vainly attempts to imitate. When she opened her mouth, you perceived the beauty of pearls, and the sweetness of roses. She was full of graces. Nothing was so soft as her looks, so modest as her carriage, so touching as the sound of her voice. An air of gayety and tenderness breathed around her; but so pure and happily tempered, as to inspire every beholder with the sentiments of virtue; for she was chaste as the spangled dewdrop on the thorn. Such was the description given of this divine creature by her enslaved lover. But, unfortunately for his happiness, she was at this time married to Hugues de Sade, whose family was originally of Avignon, and held the first offices there. Notwithstanding the sufferings he underwent from the natural agitation of an affection so tender as that which now engrossed his soul, he owns that Laura behaved to him with kindness so long as he concealed his passion; but when she discovered that he was captivated with her charms, she treated him with great severity; avoiding every place it was likely he would frequent, and concealing her face under a large veil whenever they accidentally met. The whole soul of Petrarch was overthrown by this disastrous passion; and he felt all the visitation of unfortunate love as grievously as if it had been founded upon less virtuous principles. He endeavored to calm and tranquillize the troubles of his breast by retiring to the celebrated solitude of Vaucluse, a place in which nature delighted to appear under a form the most singular and romantic; "But, alas!" says he, "I knew not what I was doing. The resource was ill suited to the safety I sought. Solitude was incapable of mitigating the severity of my sorrows. The griefs that hung around my heart, consumed me like a devouring flame. I had no means of flying from their attacks. I was alone, without consolation, and in the deepest distress, without even the counsel of a friend to assist me. Melancholy and despair shot their poisoned arrows against my defenceless breast, and I filled the unsoothing and romantic vale with my sighs and lamentations. The muse indeed, conveyed my sufferings to the world; but while the poet was praised, the unhappy lover remained unpitied and forlorn."

The love which inspired the lays of Petrarch was a pure and perfect passion of the heart; and his sufferings were rendered peculiarly poignant by a melancholy sense of the impossibility of ever being united with the object of it; but the love of Abelard and Eloisa was a furious heat of wild desire. This passion flows clear or muddied, peaceful or violent, in proportion to the sources from which it springs. When it arises from pure and unpolluted sources, its stream is clear, peaceful, and surrounded with delights: but when its source is foul, and its course improperly directed, it foams and rages, overswells its banks, and destroys the scenes which nature intended it to fertilize and adorn. The different effects produced by the different kinds of this powerful passion, have, on observing how differently the character of the same person appears when influenced by the one or the other of them, given rise to an idea that the human species are possessed of two souls; the one leading to vice, and the other conducting to virtue. A celebrated philosopher has illustrated this notion by the following story:

A virtuous young prince, of an heroic soul, capable of love and friendship, made war upon a tyrant, who was in every respect his reverse. It was the happiness of our prince to be as great a conqueror by his clemency and bounty, as by his arms and military virtue. Already he had won over to his party several potentates and princes, who had before been subject to the tyrant. Among those who still adhered to the enemy there was a prince, who, having all the advantages of person and merit, had lately been made happy in the possession and mutual love of the most beautiful princess in the world. It happened that the occasion of the war called the new married prince to a distance from his beloved princess. He left her secure as he thought, in a strong castle, far within the country; but, in his absence, the place was taken by surprise, and the princess brought a captive to the quarters of the heroic prince. There was in the camp a young nobleman the favorite of the prince; one who had been educated with him, and was still treated by him with perfect familiarity. Him he immediately sent for, and with strict injunctions, committed the captive princess to his charge; resolving she should be treated with that respect which was due to her rank and merit. It was the same young lord who had discovered her disguised among the prisoners, and learnt her story; the particulars of which he now related to the prince. He spoke in ecstacy on this occasion; telling the prince how beautiful she appeared even in the midst of sorrow; and though disguised under the meanest habit, yet how distinguished by her air and manner from every other beauty of her sex. But what appeared strange to our young nobleman was, that the prince, during this whole relation, discovered not the least intention of seeing the lady, or satisfying that curiosity which seemed so natural on such an occasion. He pressed him, but without success. "Not see her, sir!" said he wondering, "when she is so much handsomer than any woman you have yet seen!" "For that very reason," replied the prince, "I would rather decline the interview; for should I, upon this bare report of her beauty, be so charmed as to make the first visit at this urgent time of business, I may upon sight, with better reason, be induced, perhaps, to visit her when I am more at leisure; and so again and again, until at last I may have no leisure left for my affairs." "Would you, sir, persuade me then," said the young nobleman, smiling, "that a fair face can have such power as to force the will itself, and constrain a man in any respect to act contrary to what he thinks becoming him? Are we to hearken to the poets, in what they tell us of that incendiary love and his irresistible flames? A real flame, we see, burns all alike; but that imaginary one of beauty hurts only those that are consenting. It affects no otherwise than as we ourselves are pleased to allow it. In many cases we absolutely command it, as when relation and consanguinity are in the nearest degree. Authority and law we see can master it; but it would be vain, as well as unjust, for any law to intermeddle or prescribe, was not the case voluntary, and our will entirely free." "How comes it then," replied the prince, "that if we are thus masters of our choice, and free at first to admire and love where we approve, we cannot afterward as well cease to love whenever we see cause? This latter liberty you will hardly defend; for I doubt not you have heard of many who, though they were used to set the highest value on liberty before they loved, yet, afterward, were necessitated to serve in the most abject manner, finding themselves constrained, and bound by a stronger chain than any of iron or of adamant." "Such wretches," replied the youth, "I have often heard complain, who, if you will believe them, are wretched indeed, without means or power to help themselves. You may hear them in the same manner complain grievously of life itself; but though there are doors enough at which to go out of life, they find it convenient to keep still where they are. They are the very same pretenders who, through this plea of irresistible necessity, make bold with what is another's, and attempt unlawful beds; but the law, I perceive, makes bold with them in its turn, as with other invaders of property. Neither is it your custom, sir, to pardon such offences. So that beauty itself, you must allow, is innocent and harmless, and cannot compel any one to do amiss. The debauched compel themselves, and unjustly charge their guilt on love. They who are honest and just can admire and love whatever is beautiful, without offering at any thing beyond what is allowed. How then is it possible, sir, that one of your virtue should be in pain on any such account, or fear such a temptation? You see, sir, I am sound and whole after having beheld the princess. I have conversed with her; I have admired her in the highest degree; yet I am myself still, and in my duty, and shall be ever in the same manner at your command." "It is well," replied the prince; "keep yourself so: be ever the same man, and look to your fair charge carefully, as becomes you; for it may so happen, in the present situation of the war that this beautiful captive may stand us in good stead." The young nobleman then departed to execute his commission; and immediately took such care of the captive princess that she seemed as perfectly obeyed, and had every thing which belonged to her in as great splendor as in her own principality, and in the height of her fortune. He found her in every respect deserving, and saw in her a generosity of soul exceeding even her other charms. His studies to oblige her and to soften her distress, made her, in return, desirous to express her gratitude. He soon discovered the feelings of her mind; for she showed, on every occasion, a real concern for his interest; and when he happened to fall ill, she took such tender care of him herself, and by her servants, that he seemed to owe his recovery entirely to her friendship. From these beginnings, insensibly, and by natural degrees, as may easily be conceived, the youth fell desperately in love. At first he offered not to make the least mention of his passion to the princess, for he scarce dared believe it himself. But time, and the increasing ardor of his passion, subdued his fears, and she received his declaration with an unaffected trouble, and real concern. She reasoned with him as a friend, and endeavored to persuade him to subdue so improper and extravagant a flame. But in a short time he became outrageous, and talked to her of *force*. The princess was alarmed by his audacity, and immediately sent to the prince to implore his protection. The prince received the information with the appearance of more than ordinary attention; sent instantly for one of his first ministers, and directed him to return with the princess' domestic, and tell the young nobleman that *force* was not to be used to such a lady; but that he might use *persuasion*, if he thought it was proper so to do. The minister, who was of course the inveterate enemy of his prince's favorite, aggravated the message, inveighed publicly against the young nobleman for the grossness of his misconduct, and even reproached him to his face with having been a traitor to the confidence of his prince, and a disgrace to his nation. The minister, in short, conveyed the message of his master in such virulent and angry terms, that the youth looked on his case as desperate; fell into the deepest melancholy; and prepared himself for that fate which he was conscious he well deserved. While he was thus impressed with a sense of his misconduct, and the danger to which it had exposed him, the prince commanded him to attend a private audience. The youth entered the closet of the prince covered with the deepest confusion. "I find," said he, "that I am now become dreadful to you indeed, since you can neither see me without shame, nor imagine me to be without resentment. But away with all these thoughts from this time forward! I know how much you have suffered on this occasion. I know the power of love; and am no otherwise safe myself, than by keeping out of the way of beauty. I alone am to blame; for it was I who unhappily matched you with that unequal adversary; who gave you that impracticable task; who imposed on you that hard adventure, which no one yet was ever strong enough to accomplish." "In this, sir, as in all else," replied the youth, "you express that goodness which is so natural to you. You have compassion, and can allow for human frailties; but the rest of mankind will never cease to upbraid me: nor shall I ever be forgiven, even were I able ever to forgive myself. I am reproached by my nearest friends; and I must be odious to all mankind wherever I am known. The least punishment I can think due to me is banishment for ever from your presence; for I am no longer worthy of being called your friend." "You must not think of banishing yourself for ever," replied the prince: "but trust me, if you will retire only for a while, I shall so order matters, that you shall return with the applause even of those who are now your enemies, when they find what a considerable service you shall have rendered both to them and me." Such a hint was sufficient to revive the spirits of the despairing youth. He was transported to think that his misfortunes could be turned in any way to the advantage of his prince. He entered with joy into the scheme his royal friend had contrived for the purpose of restoring him to his former fame and happiness, and appeared eager to depart and execute the directions that were given to him. "Can you then," said the prince, "resolve to quit the charming princess?" "O, sir," replied the youth, with tears in his eyes, "I am now well satisfied that I have in reality within me two distinct separate souls. This lesson of philosophy I have learnt from that villanous sophister love; for it is impossible to believe that, having one and the same soul, it should be actually both good and bad; passionate for virtue and vice, desirous of contraries. No; there must of necessity be two; and when the good soul prevails, we are happy; but when the bad prevails, we are miserable. Such was my case. Lately the ill soul was wholly master, and I was miserable; but now the good prevails, by your assistance, and I am plainly a new creature, with quite another apprehension, another reason, and another will."

He who would be master of his appetites, must not only avoid temptation, but vigilantly restrain the earliest shoots of fancy, and destroy the first blooms of a warm imagination. It is the very nature of confidence to be always in danger. To permit the mind to riot in scenes of fancied delights, under an idea that reason will be able to extinguish the flames of desire, is to nurse and foster the sensual appetites, which, when guided by the cool and temperate voice of nature alone, are seldom raised to an improper height. The natural current of the blood, even in the warmest constitutions, and under the most torrid zone, would keep an even, temperate course, were it not accelerated by such incentives. Youth indeed despises this species of reasoning, and imputes it to the sickness of satiety, or the coldness of old age. I have, however, in general, observed, that those who seek these incitements to what they improperly call love, possess a rayless eye, a hollow cheek, a palsied hand, a pallid countenance; and these symptoms of faded splendour and withered strength, unquestionably prove that they have not consulted nature in their gay pursuits; for nature has not planted any propensities in the human frame which lead it to early ruin, or premature decay. The blame which is so unjustly thrown upon temperament and constitution, belongs to the indulgence of false and clamorous passions, those which sensual fancies, and lascivious ideas have raised to the destruction of chastity and health.

Monastic institutions produce, in this respect, incalculable mischiefs. The sexes, whom these religious prisons seclude from the free and unconfined intercourses of society, suffer their imaginations to riot without restraint or discipline, in proportion to the violence imposed on their actions. A thousand boyish fancies, eager appetites and warm desires, are perpetually playing truant, and the chastity of the soul is corrupted. To effect the conquest of the passion of love, it is absolutely necessary that the evil suggestions of the imagination should be first silenced; and he who succeeds in quelling the insurrections of that turbulent inmate, or in quieting its commotions, achieves an enterprise at once difficult and glorious. The holy Jerome checked the progress of many disorderly passions which he found rising in his breast; but the passion of love resisted all his opposition, and followed him, with increasing fury, even into the frightful cavern to which he retired to implore, in humble prayer and solitary abstraction, the mercies of his God. The solitude, however remote, to which the demon of sensuality is admitted, is soon crowded with legions of tormenting fiends. John, the anchorite of the deserts of Thebais, wisely addressed his solitary brethren, "If there be any among you who in his pride, conceives that he has entirely renounced the devil and all his works, he should learn that it is not sufficient to have done this merely by his lips, by having resigned his worldly dignities, and by dividing his possessions among the poor; for, unless he has also abandoned his sensual appetites, his salvation cannot be secure. It is only by purifying our bosoms from the pernicious influence of this master passion, that we can ever hope to counteract the machinations of satan, and to guard our hearts from his dangerous practices. Sin always introduces itself under the guidance of some guilty passion; some fond desire; some pleasing inclination, which we willingly indulge, and by that means suffer the enemy of peace to establish his unruly dominion in our souls. Then tranquillity and real happiness quit their abode in our hearts, and all is uproar and anarchy within. This must be the fate of all who permit an evil spirit to seat itself on the throne of their hearts, and to scatter around the poisonous seeds of wild desire and vicious inclinations." But love once indulged in bright and rapturous fancies, fills the mind with such high and transporting ideas of supreme bliss, that the powers of reason are seldom, if ever, capable of making head against its fascinations. The hermit and the monk, who, from the nature of their situations, cannot taste its real charms, ought, if it were for that reason alone, to stifle at their birth the earliest emotions of this inspiring passion; for the indulgence of it must prove fatal to the virtue, and of course destructive to the peace of every recluse. The impossibility that such characters can listen with any propriety to the dictates of this delightful passion, shows in the strongest manner the impolicy and absurdity of those institutions, on the members of which celibacy is enjoined. The happiness of every individual, as well as the civil and religious interests of society, are best promoted by inducing the endearments of sense to improve the sympathies, tenderness, and affections of the human heart. But these blessings are denied to the solitary fanatic, who is condemned to endure the suppression of his passions, and prevented from indulging without endangering his principles, both the desires of sense, and the dreams of fancy. He cannot form that delightful union of the sexes, where sentiments of admiration are increased by prospects of personal advantage; where private enjoyment arises from a sense of mutual merit; and the warmest beams of love are tempered by the refreshing gales of friendship. The grosser parts of this innate and glowing passion can alone occupy his fancy; and the sentiments it instils, instead of refining his desires, and meliorating his affections, tend, through the operation of his soul and corrupted imagination, to render his appetites still more depraved. He is as ignorant of its benefits as he is of its chaste and dignified pleasures; and totally unacquainted with its fine sensibilities, and varied emotions, his bosom burns with the most violent rage; his mind wallows in images of sensuality; and his temper frets itself, by unjustly accusing the tempter as the author of his misery. If the luxurious cogitations of such a character were dissipated by the pleasures and pursuits of busy life; if the violence of his passions were checked by laborious exercises; and if habits of rational study enabled him to vary the uniformity of retirement, and to substitute the excursions of mental curiosity, and moral reflections, instead of that perpetual recurrence of animal desire by which he is infected, the danger we have described would certainly be reduced; but without such aids, his self-denials, his penitence, his prayers, and all the austere discipline of the monkish and ascetic school, will be ineffectual. Celibacy, indeed, instead of assisting, as their disciples mistakingly conceive, to clear the soul from its earthly impurities, and to raise it to divine brightness and sublimity, drags it down to the basest appetites and lowest desires. But matrimony, or that suitable and appropriate union of the sexes which prevails under different circumstances, according to the manner and custom of different societies, leads, when properly formed, to the highest goal of human bliss.

The mischievous effects which the celibacy and solitude of monastic institutions produce on that passion which arises so spontaneously between the sexes in the human heart, will appear unavoidable, when it is considered how absurdly the founders of these religious retreats have frequently endeavored to guard against the danger. The partitions which divide virtues from their opposite vices are so slender and conjoined, that we scarcely reach the limits of the one before we enter to a certain degree, the confines of the other. How ridiculous, therefore, is it to conceive, that frequent meditation on forbidden pleasures, should be at all likely to eradicate impure ideas from the mind. And yet the Egyptian monastics were enjoined to have these rules constantly in their contemplation: first, that their bosoms must remain unagitated by the thoughts of love; that they should never permit their fancies to loiter on voluptuous images; that female beauty, in its fairest form, and most glowing charms, should be incapable of exciting in their hearts the least sensation; and that, even during the hours of sleep, their minds should continue untainted by such impure affections. The chastity of these solitary beings was, on some occasions, actually tried by experiment; but the consequences which resulted from such irrational discipline, were directly the reverse of those it was intended to produce. The imagination was vitiated, and the inclination rendered so corrupt, that neither the examples nor the precepts of the more enlightened ages were able to correct their manners, or reclaim them from the machinations of the unclean spirit.

Numberless indeed, and horrid, are the instances recorded by Ruffinus, and other writers, of the perversions of all sense and reason, of all delicacy and refinement, of all virtue and true holiness, which prevailed in the ascetic solitudes of every description, while the nuptial state was held incompatible with the duties of religion, and the sexes separated from each other, that they might more piously, and with less interruption, follow its dictates. Some of the fathers of the church defined female celibacy to be the only means of living a chaste and godly life amidst the impurities of a sinful world, and regaining, during the perdition of gross mortality, the resemblance of the soul's celestial origin. The holy, happy tie of matrimony they considered as a cloak to the indulgence of impure desires, and launched their anathemas against it as an hateful institution. Even the eloquent and pious Chrysostom says, "that a double purpose was intended to be attained by the institution of marriage, *viz.* the propagation of the species, and the gratification of sexual affection; but that, as population had sufficiently covered the face of the earth, the first had become no longer necessary; and that it was the duty of the sexes rather to conquer their affections by abstinence and prayer, than indulge them under so thin a disguise." The human soul, he admits, must, in a state of celibacy, subsist under a perpetual warfare and the faculties be in continual ferment; but contends, that piety exists in proportion to the difficulties which the sufferer surmounts. The holy fathers seem, from the whole strain of their exhortations and reasonings, to have considered female chastity in a very serious point of view; and there can be no doubt but that it is the brightest jewel and most becoming ornament of the sex; but these reverend teachers were so blinded by their zeal, that they lost all sight of nature, and mistakingly conceived that the Great Creator had planted affections in our hearts, and passions in our breasts, only to try our tempers in suppressing their turbulence, rather than promote our happiness, and to answer the ends of his creation, by a sober and rational indulgence of them.

But nature will not be argued out of her rights; and these absurd doctrines introduced into every monastic institution throughout Europe a private intercourse, hostile, from its evil example to the interests both of morality and religion. The nuns of the convent of Argenteuil, who chose Eloisa for their Abbess, were in all probability, influenced in their choice by the recollections of her former frailty, and their knowledge of the present ruling passion of her heart; they meant to provide the abbey with a superior who, if she were not inclined to promote, would feel no disposition to interrupt their intrigues. The fact certainly was, that during the time Eloisa presided over the convent, the conduct of the nuns was so extremely licentious, that Sugger, abbot of St. Dennis, complained of their irregularities to Pope Honorius, in such a manner as to induce his holiness to give the abbot possession of it; and he immediately expelled the negligent prioress and her intriguing sisters, and established in their place a monastery of his own order. Strong suspicions may, perhaps, prevail against the virtue and integrity of Eloisa's character, from the dissoluteness which existed in this society; but she was certainly not included by name in the articles of accusation which the abbot of St. Dennis transmitted upon this subject to the court of Rome; and there is every reason to believe that these irregularities were carefully concealed from her knowledge. When this lovely victim was presented with the veil, some persons who pitied her youth, and admired her beauty, represented to her the cruel sacrifice she would make of herself by accepting it: but she immediately exclaimed, in the words of Cornelia, after the death of Pompey the great—

> "Oh my loved lord! our fatal marriage draws
>
> On thee this doom, and I the guilty cause:
>
> Then while thou go'st th' extremes of fate to prove,
>
> I'll share that fate, and expiate thus my love!"

and accepted the fatal present with a constancy not to have been expected in a woman who had so high a taste for pleasures which she might still enjoy. It will therefore, be easily conceived, that her distress, on being ignominiously expelled from this retreat, was exceedingly severe. She applied to Abelard to procure her some permanent asylum, where she might have the opportunity of estranging herself from all earthly weaknesses and passions; and he, by the permission of the bishop of Troyes, resigned to her the house and the chapel of Paraclete, with its appendages, where she settled with a few sisters, and became herself the foundress of a nunnery. Of this monastery she continued the superior until she died; and whatever her conduct was among the licentious nuns of Argenteuil, she lived so regular in this her new and last retreat, and conducted herself with such exemplary prudence, zeal, and piety, that all her former failings were forgot, her character adored by all who knew her, and her monastery in a short time enriched with so great a variety of donations, that she was celebrated as the ablest cultivator of the virtues of forgiveness and Christian charity then existing. The bishop of the district behaved to her as if she had been his own daughter; the neighboring priors and abbots treated her with all the tenderness and attention of a real sister: and those who were distressed and poor, revered her as their mother. But all her cares, and all her virtues, could not protect her against the returning weakness of her heart. "Solitude," says she, "is insupportable to a mind that is ill at ease; its troubles increase in the midst of silence, and retirement heightens them. Since I have been shut up within these walls, I have done nothing but weep for our misfortunes:

this cloister has resounded with my cries, and like a wretch condemned to eternal slavery, I have worn out my days in grief and sighing."

The useful regulations imposed by the wisdom of St. Benedict upon the votaries of monastic retirement, were soon neglected. Abstinence and prayer were succeeded by luxury and impiety. The revenues of the several orders had, by the increased value of property, become so great, that they were expended in purchasing a remission of those duties which their founders had enjoined. The admission of the poor laity relieved the initiated members from the toil of cultivating the demesne lands, and produced a system of indolence and laziness. They exchanged their long fast and unsavory diet, for frequent feasts, and the richest repasts; substituted indolent pride for laborious humility; and lost entirely their original piety and virtue. Abelard, indeed, and some few other abbots of the tenth century, endeavored to restore the ancient discipline, but they were reviled and persecuted with the most vindictive malice by their contemporaries. The duke of Brittany, in order to secure Abelard from the rage with which he was pursued, for exercising qualities which ought to have procured him admiration and esteem, gave him the convent of St. Gildas, as an asylum from their hatred. The high character which this monastery comparatively enjoyed for regularity and good order, excited a hope that he might there find rest from his vexations, and consolation for his griefs. But instead of finding it the seat of wisdom and piety, and the mansion of tranquillity, he discovered the most dissolute manners and abandoned conduct prevailing in every part of the convent. His mild and rational attempts to reclaim these disorderly brethren, were so far from producing the desired effect upon their minds, that it only provoked their rage, and gave new edge to their malice. Foiled in their endeavors, by conspiracy and calumny, to dispossess him of his situation, they attempted, several times at their common repasts, to infuse poison into his victuals: and at length, dreadful to relate! actually administered, in the sacramental cup, the poisoned chalice to his lips, but which he was miraculously prevented from tasting. It is, indeed, impossible to read the description he has given of his dreadful situation in this wild and savage community, without shuddering at the idea how much an irrational solitude tends to corrupt the manners and deprave the heart. "I live," says he, in his letter to Philintus, "in a barbarous country, the language of which I do not understand. I have no conversation but with the rudest people. My walks are on the inaccessible shore of a sea which is perpetually stormy. My monks are only known by their dissoluteness, and living without any rule or order. Ah! Philintus, were you to see my habitation, you would rather think it a slaughter house than a convent. The doors and walks are without any ornament except the heads of wild boars, the antlers of stags, the feet of foxes and the hides of other animals, which are nailed up against them. The cells are hung with the skins of victims destroyed in the chase. The monks have not so much as a bell to wake them, and are only roused from their drowsiness by the howling of dogs and the croaking of ravens. Nothing disturbs their laziness or languor but the rude noises of hunting; and their only alternatives are riot and rest. But I should return my thanks to heaven if that were their only fault. I endeavor in vain to recall them to their duty; they all combine against me; and I only expose myself to continual vexations and dangers. I imagine I see every moment a naked sword hanging over my head. Sometimes they surround me, and load me with the vilest abuse; and even when they abandon me, I am still left to my own dreadful tormenting thoughts." This single example would be sufficient to prove the extraordinary dominion which solitude has over the human mind. It is, indeed, unless it be managed with great good sense, the complete nursery of mischief. The mind is without those numerous incentives to action which are continually occurring in the busy world; and nothing can contribute to produce irregular and disorderly passions more than the want of some pursuit by which the heart is interested and the mind employed. The minds of idle persons are always restless; their hearts never at perfect ease; their spirits continually on the fret; and their passions goaded to the most unwarrantable excess.

Idleness, even in social life, inflicts the severest torments on the soul; destroys the repose of individuals; and, when general, frequently endangers the safety of the state. Timotheus, an Egyptian monk, surnamed the Cat, a short time after the Eutychian Controversy, in the year 457, felt an ambition to fill the episcopal and patriarchal chair. The splenetic restlessness which prevailed among the monks in their several monastic solitudes, seemed to present to his observing eye proper instruments for the execution of his scheme. He was conscious, from his profound knowledge of the human character, that if men who had so long remained in uneasy and dissatisfied indolence, could be provoked to activity, their zeal would be as turbulent as their former life had been lazy and supine; and that their dispositions might be easily turned to the accomplishment of his wishes. The better to effect his purpose, he clothed himself in a white garment, crept silently in the dead of night to the cells of his companions, and, through a tube, which concealed his voice while it magnified the sound of it, hailed every monk by his name. The sound seemed to convey the voice of heaven to the superstitious ears of the awakened auditors; and the sagacious and enterprising trumpeter did not fail to announce himself as an ambassador of heaven, sent in the name of the Almighty to command the monks to assemble immediately, to consult on the most likely mode of deposing the Nestorian heretic Proterus, and of raising the favored and orthodox Timotheus to the episcopal throne. The idea of being thus elected to execute this pious rebellion, roused all the sleeping powers of these solitary and hitherto idle fanatics; they rose tumultuously at the sacred signal; proclaimed him as a heaven elected patriarch; solicited him with friendly violence, not to refuse the promised boon; and burning with all the ardor of expected success, marched, in a few days under the banner of the imposter, to Alexandria, where they inspired the members of other monasteries with their own delusion, and created throughout Egypt the wildest and most tremendous commotions. The populace caught the religious frenzy, and joined in vast numbers the monastic rout. Assisted by this desperate rabble, Timotheus proceeded to the principal church of Alexandria, where he was, by a preconcerted arrangement, pompously received by two deposed bishops, and ordained the metropolitan of the whole Egyptian territory. Proterus was astonished at this sudden irruption, and hurled his anathemas with great art and dexterity against the impious audacity of the obscure monastic who had thus dared to depart from the humility of his station, and to invade with his indolent brethren, the rights of sovereignty; but being well aware of the fury with which this description of men generally act when they are once set in motion, and being informed of the vast multitude by which they had been joined, he thought it prudent to quit his palace, and to retire to the sacred shelter of the church of St. Quirinus. Heathens and barbarians had heretofore respected this venerable sanctuary; but, upon the present occasion, it was incapable of giving safety to its aged refugee. The furious troops of the holy imposter burst with irresistible violence through the walls of this consecrated edifice, and with their daggers drank the blood of the innocent pontiff, even upon that altar, the very sight of which ought to have paralyzed the hand of guilt. His surrounding and numerous friends, particularly six ecclesiastics of great eminence, learning, and piety, shared the fate of their unhappy master, and were found, when the dreadful massacre was over, clinging with fondness, in the arms of death, round his mangled body. But it was necessary for the murderers to calumniate the purity of that life which they had thus violently and injuriously destroyed. They accordingly dragged the corpse of this virtuous patriarch to the most public part of the city, and, after the grossest abuse of his character, and most scandalous misrepresentation of his conduct, hung it on an elevated cross, and exposed it to the brutal insults of the misguided and deluded populace. To complete this unmanly outrage, they at length committed the torn and mangled remains of this excellent prelate to the flames, and hurled his ashes, amidst the most opprobrious and insulting epithets, into the darkened air; exclaiming with horrid imprecations, that the mortal part of such a wretch was not entitled to the right of sepulchre, or even the tears of friends. So furious and undaunted, indeed, were all the oriental monks, when once roused from their monastic lethargy, that even the soldiers of the Greek emperors cautiously avoided meeting them in the field. The fury by which they were actuated was so blind, that the pious Chrysostom, the warmest and most zealous advocate for monastic institutions, trembled at his approach. This celebrated father of the church was born in the year 344, of one of the first families of the city of Antioch, and added new lustre to their fame by his virtues and his eloquence. Having finished his studies with wonderful success, under Libanus, the greatest rhetorician of the age, he devoted himself to the study of the law; but religion having planted itself deeply in his mind, he quitted all secular concerns, and retired into solitude among the mountains in the vicinity of the city, where, in the dreary caves, he devoted two entire years to penitence and prayer. Ill health, however, obliged him to return to Antioch; he began to preach the Word, and was soon followed by a host of disciples. The life of this excellent pastor was an example to his whole flock. He endeavored to drive away the wolves from the folds, and sent missionaries even into Scythia, to convert its inhabitants to Christianity. These missions, and his various charities, required either considerable revenues or the most rigid economy; and the holy patriarch was contented to live in the extremest poverty, that he might have the better opportunity of relieving the sufferings of his fellow creatures. The character and conduct of this virtuous pontiff soon gained him the hearts of his people, and he set himself earnestly to reform the many abuses which at this time prevailed at Constantinople. The severity and vehemence, however, with which he declaimed against the pride, the luxury, and the rapacity of the great; the zeal with which he endeavored to reform the vices and misconduct of the clergy; and the eagerness he discovered for the conversion of heretics, created him a multitude of enemies; and Eutropius, the favorite of the Emperor Arcadius; Gainas, the tyrant to whom he had refused protection for the Arians; Theophilus, of Alexandria, the patron of the Origenists; and the disciples of Arius, whom he banished from Constantinople, entered into a conspiracy against him; and an occasion soon happened, which gave them the opportunity of taking ample vengeance. The intrepid preacher, convinced that while he declaimed against vice in general, the peculiar vices which prevailed in the court of the Empress Eudoxia, and the personal misconduct of the Empress herself, called aloud for his severest animadversions, he took every opportunity of exposing them to the public abhorrence. The resentment of the court encouraged the discontent of the clergy and monks of Constantinople, who had been very severely disciplined by the zeal of the archbishop. He had condemned from the pulpit the domestic females of the clergy of Constantinople, who, under the name of servants or sisters, afforded a perpetual occasion either of sin or scandal. The silent and solitary ascetics, who had secluded themselves from the world, were entitled to the warmest appprobation of Chrysostom; but he despised and stigmatized, as the disgrace of their holy profession, the crowd of degenerate monks, who from some unworthy motives of pleasure or profit, so frequently infested the streets of the metropolis. To the voice of persuasion, the archbishop was obliged to add the lesson of authority; and in his visitation through the Asiatic provinces, he deposed thirteen bishops of Lydia and Phrygia; and declared that a deep corruption of simony and licentiousness had infected the whole episcopal order. These bishops also entered into the confederacy above mentioned, and the excellent Chrysostom was studiously represented as the intolerable tyrant of the eastern church. This ecclesiastical conspiracy was managed by the archbishop of Alexandria, who, by the invitation of Eudoxia, landed at Constantinople with a stout body of Egyptian mariners, to encounter the populace, and a train of dependant bishops, to secure, by their voices, a majority of a synod. The synod was convened in the suburbs of Chalcedon, and was called the Oak; in which Chrysostom, was accused of treason against the empress; rudely arrested, and driven into exile; from whence, however, he was in two days recalled; but, upon a repetition of his imputed offences, was again banished to the remote and desolate town of Cucusus among the ridges of mount Taurus, in the Lesser Armenia. On his way to this place, he was detained by sickness at Cesarea, and at length confined to his bed. The bishop of Cesarea, who had long entertained a secret enmity against him, unmoved by his fallen fortunes and helpless state, stirred up the lazy monks of the surrounding monasteries to vengeance against him. The fury with which they issued from their respective cells was incredible; like the sleeping powder of the present age, they burst into immediate conflagration and explosion at the touch of that hand by which they were fired, and directing their heated animosity against the dying Chrysostom, surrounded his house and threatened, that if he did not immediately depart, they would involve it in flames, and bury him in its ruins. The soldiers of the garrison were called out to protect the life of this virtuous ecclesiastic; and, on their arrival at the scene of action, very courteously requested the enraged monks to be quiet and depart; but the request was treated with contempt and defiance; and it was by the humane resolution of Chrysostom himself that this tumult was quelled; for, rather than the blood of his fellow creatures should be shed on his account, he desired a litter might be procured, into which, in his almost expiring state, he was roughly laid, and, by his departure from the city, escaped the fury which thus assailed his life. It is evident, from these facts, that the irrational solitude of monastic institutions, particularly that which prevailed in the early ages of Christianity in the eastern parts of the converted world, instead of rendering the votaries of it mild, complacent and humane, filled their minds with the wildest notions, and the most uncharitable and acrimonious passions, and fostered in their hearts the most dangerous and destructive vices. It is truly said, by a very elegant writer and profound observer of men and manners, that monastic institutions unavoidably contract and fetter the human mind; that the partial attachment of a monk to the interest of his order, which is often incompatible with that of other citizens, the habit of implicit obedience to the will of a superior, together with the frequent return of the wearisome and frivolous duties of the cloister, debase his faculties, and extinguish that generosity of sentiment and spirit which qualifies men for thinking and feeling justly, with respect to what is proper in life and conduct; and that father Paul of Venice was, perhaps, the only person educated in a cloister, that ever was altogether superior to its prejudices, or who viewed the transactions of men, and reasoned concerning the interests of society, with the enlarged sentiments of a philosopher, with the discernment of a man conversant in affairs, and with the liberality of a gentleman. Depraved, however, as this order of men has ever been, it was to their prayers and masses that all the princes and potentates of more than half the discovered regions of the earth confided their salvation, and expected from their intercession, divine favor from the fountain of all goodness and truth. But the fears which these artful and intriguing ecclesiastics raised in the weak or guilty minds of their contemporaries, instead of being quieted by the conciliatory and comforting doctrines of the gospel of Christ, were converted to the purposes of their own sordid avarice, and made subservient to the enjoyment of their vices, and the advancement of their power. They inculcated the notion, that the surest passport to eternal bliss was to overwhelm them with riches, and to indulge them with extraordinary privileges; and every haughty noble, or despotic sovereign, who was anxious to gratify his own wanton pleasures, and capricious vices, at the expense of his people's prosperity and happiness, endeavored to reconcile himself to his offended God, by bribing these ambitious and greedy monastics to grant them absolution for their deepest crimes. Their history exhibits, in full view, the melancholy truth, that their hearts were corrupted by the worst passions that disgrace humanity, and that the discipline of the convent was seldom productive of a single virtue. Enthusiasts, indeed, of every description, whose sentiments and feelings are continually at war with the dictates of nature, and who renounce all the pleasing sympathies, gentle endearments, kind connexions, and rational enjoyments of life, are not likely to entertain any great anxiety for the interest or happiness of others, or to feel the least commiseration for their sorrows. Occupied by sordid and selfish pursuits, they must hate and despise a society, to the lively enjoyments of which they look back with such keen regret. When the mind, alas! has numbed its sense of social joys, and become a stranger to the delightful charms of sweet domestic love; when all affection for the world and its concerns has been studiously expelled from the bosom, and no kind feeling or social inclination suffered to fill the vacant heart; when man has separated himself from his species, and has not united his soul with his Creator, he has lost all power of being happy himself, or of communicating happiness to others.

The bishop exceeded the inferior clergy in every kind of profligacy, as much as in opulence and power; and, of course, their superintending and visitorial authority was not exerted to lessen or restrain the prevalence of those vices which their evil example contributed so greatly to increase. Time and chance sometimes produce extraordinary events; and if a really pious, vigilant, and austere prelate arose amidst the general dissoluteness of the age, his single effort to reclaim these solitary ecclesiastics was seldom attended with success. These fathers, indeed, frequently scrutinized with great minuteness into the practices of the convents; and as they were not so able to detect the guilt of incontinency, as some philosophers of the present age pretend to be, by the lines and features of the face, they proceeded upon evidence less delicate, perhaps, but certainly more demonstrative and unerring.

The celebrated Boccace has, by his witty and ingenious tales, very severely satirized the licentiousness and immorality which prevailed during his time in the Italian monasteries; but, by exposing the scandalous lives, and lashing the vices, of the monks, nuns, and other orders of the Catholic clergy, he has been decried as a contemner of religion, and as an enemy to true piety. Contemporary historians have also delivered the most disgusting accounts of their intemperance and debauchery. The frailty, indeed, of the female monastics was even an article of regular taxation; and the holy father did not disdain to fill his coffers with the price of their impurities. The frail nun, whether she had become immured within a convent, or still resided without its walls, might redeem her lost honor, and be reinstated in her former dignity and virtue, for a few ducats. This scandalous traffic was carried to an extent that soon destroyed all sense of morality, and heightened the hue of vice. Ambrosius, bishop of Camadoli, a prelate of extraordinary virtue, visited various convents in his diocese, but, on inspecting their proceedings, he found no traces of virtue, or even of decency remaining in any one of them; nor was he able, with all the sagacity he exercised on the subject, to reinfuse the smallest particle of these qualities into the degenerated minds of the sisterhood.

The reform of the nunneries was the first step that distinguished the government of Sextus IV. after he ascended the papal throne, at the close of the fifteenth century. Bossus, a celebrated canon, of the strictest principles, and most inflexible disposition, was the agent selected by his holiness for this arduous achievement. The Genoese convents, where the nuns lived in open defiance of all the rules of decency and precepts of religion, were the first objects of his attention. The orations which he publicly uttered from the pulpit, as well as the private lectures and exhortations which he delivered to the nuns from the confessional chair, were fine models, not only of his zeal and probity, but of his literature and eloquence. They breathed, in the most impressive manner, the true spirit of Christian purity; but his glowing representations of the bright beauties of virtue, and the dark deformities of vice made little impression upon their corrupt hearts. Despising the open calumnies of the envious, and the secret hostilities of the guilty, he proceeded, in spite of all discouragement and opposition, in his highly honorable pursuit; and at length, by his wisdom and assiduity, beheld the fairest prospects of success daily opening to his view. The rays of hope, however, had scarcely beamed upon his endeavors, when they were immediately overclouded by disappointment. The arm of magistracy, which he had wisely called upon to aid the accomplishment of his design, was enervated by the venality of its hand; and the incorrigible objects of his solicitude having freed themselves by bribery from the terror of the civil power, contemned the reformer's denunciation of eternal vengeance hereafter, and relapsed into their former licentiousness and depravity. A few, indeed, among the great number of nuns who inhabited these guilty convents, were converted by the force of his eloquent remonstrances, and became afterward highly exemplary by the virtue and piety of their lives; but the rest abandoned themselves to their impious courses; and though more vigorous methods were, in a short time, adopted against the refractory monastics, they set all attempts to reform them at defiance. The modes, perhaps, in which their vices were indulged, changed with the character of the age; and as manners grew more refined, the gross and shameful indulgences of the monks and nuns were changed into a more elegant and decent style of enjoyment. Fashion might render them more prudent and reserved in their intrigues; but their passions were not less vicious, nor their dispositions less corrupt.

The disorderly manners of these solitary devotees were among the principal causes that produced the reformation. There is a point beyond which even depravity cannot go in corrupting the manners of the age. The number and power of the monastics, or, as they were at that time called, the regular clergy, was certainly great, and their resistance to the approaches of reformation obstinate; but the temper of the times had changed, and the glorious and beneficial event was at length accomplished. The Catholics viewed the dismemberment of their church as a fatal stroke to their interest and power; but it has since been confessed, by every candid and rational member of this communion to be an event which has contributed to advance morals to a higher degree of perfection than they had ever before attained since the introduction of Christianity, and to restore the discipline of the church to some portion of its original purity.

The pure spirit of the gospel of Christ breathes forth a holy religion, founded on meekness, charity, kindness, and brotherly love; but fanaticism, when joined to a systematic and irrational solitude, only produces the rank and poisonous fruits we have already described. The trivial, querulous, and intolerant superstitions, which, during so many ages, eclipsed the reason and morals of mankind, and obscured, in clouds of lust and cruelty, the bright rays of evangelical truth, were the sad effects of irrational solitude. The best affections of nature were perverted or suppressed; all the gentle offices of humanity were neglected; moral sentiments despised; and the angel voice of piety unheard, or converted into the violent vociferations of hatred, and the cries of persecution. The loud clangors of pretended orthodoxy resounded with sanguinary hostilities from shore to shore; the earth was deluged with the blood of those who dared to deny, or even to doubt the absurd and idle dogmas which the monks every where invented: and their horrid barbarities were attempted to be justified by propagating the notion that severity with heretics was the only mode of preserving the true faith. Oh! how blind is human folly! How obdurate are hearts vitiated by pride! How can that be the true faith which tears asunder every social tie; annihilates all the feelings of nature; places cruelty and horror on the throne of humanity and love, and scatters ferocious fury and insatiable hatred through the paths of life? But we may now indulge a pleasing hope, that the period is at hand, when the sacred temple of religion, purified by the labors of learned and truly pious men, from the foul stains with which fanaticism and ambition have so long defaced it, shall be restored to its own divine simplicity; and only the voice of gentleness, of love, of peace of virtue, and of goodness, be heard within its walls. Then will every Christian be truly taught the only means by which his days may be useful and his life happy; and Catholics, Lutherans, Calvinists, Protestants, and every really religious class of men, will unite in acts of sincere benevolence and universal peace. No austere, gloomy, and dispiriting duties: no irrational penances and unnatural mortification, will be enjoined; no intolerant cruelties be inflicted; no unsocial institutions established; no rites of solitary selfishness be required; but reason and religion in divine perfection, will reassume their reign; and unaffected and sincere devotion will occupy every mind; the Almighty will be worshipped *in spirit* and *in truth*; and we shall be convinced that "the wicked are like the troubled sea when it cannot rest; but that the work of righteousness is peace, and the effect of righteousness, quietude and assurance for ever." To effect this, a rational retirement from the tumults of the world will be occasionally necessary, in order to *commune with our own hearts, and be still*, and to dispose our minds to such a train of thinking, as shall prepare us, when the giddy whirl of life is finished for the society of more exalted spirits.

> Oh! would mankind but make fair truth their guide,
> And force the helm from prejudice and pride,
> Were once these maxims fix'd, that God's our friend,
> Virtue our good, and happiness our end,
> How soon must reason o'er the world prevail,
> And error, fraud and superstition fail!
> None would hereafter, then, with groundless fear,
> Describe th' Almighty cruel and severe;
> Predestinating some, without pretence,
> To heaven; and some to hell, for no offence;
> Inflicting endless pains for transient crimes,
> And favoring sects or nations, men or times.
> To please him, none would foolishly forbear,
> Or food, or rest, or itch in shirts of hair:
> Or deem it merit to believe, or teach,
> What reason contradicts or cannot reach.
> None would fierce zeal for piety mistake,
> Or malice, for whatever tenet's sake;
> Or think salvation to one sect confin'd,
> And heaven too narrow to contain mankind.
> No more would brutal rage disturb our peace,
> But envy, hatred, war, and discord cease;
> Our own and others' good each hour employ,
> And all things smile with universal joy;
> Fair virtue then, with pure religion join'd,
> Would regulate and bless the human mind,
> And man be what his Maker first design'd.

Chapter VII
Of the danger of idleness in solitude

Idleness is truly said to be the root of all evil; and solitude certainly encourages in the generality of its votaries this baneful disposition. Nature has so framed the character of man, that his happiness essentially depends on his passions being properly interested, his imagination busied, and his faculties employed; but these engagements are seldom found in the vacant scenes and tedious hours of retirement from the world, except by those who have acquired the great and happy art of furnishing their own amusements; an art which, as we have already shown, can never be learnt in the irrational solitude of caves and cells.

The idleness which solitude is so apt to induce, is dangerous in proportion to the natural strength, activity, and spirit of the mind; for it is observed, that the highest characters are frequently goaded by that restlessness which accompanies leisure, to acts of the wildest outrage and greatest enormity. The ancient legislators were so conscious that indolence, whether indulged in solitude or in society, is the nurse of civil commotion, and the chief instigator of moral turpitude, that they wisely framed their laws to prevent its existence. Solon, observing that the city was filled with persons who assembled from all parts on account of the great security in which the people lived in Attica, that the country withal was poor and barren, and being conscious that merchants, who traffic by sea, do not use to transport their goods where they can have nothing in exchange, turned the attention of the citizens to manufactures; and for this purpose made a law, that he who was three times convicted of idleness, should be deemed *infamous*; that no son should be obliged to maintain his father if he had not taught him a trade; that trade should be accounted *honorable*; and that the council of the Areopagus should examine into every man's means of living, and chastise the idle with the greatest severity. Draco conceived it so necessary to prevent the prevalency of a vice to which man is by nature prone, and which is so destructive to his character, and ruinous to his manners, that he punished idleness with death. The tyrant Pisistratus, as

Theophrastus relates, was so convinced of the importance of preventing idleness among his subjects, that he made a law against it, which produced at once industry in the country, and tranquillity in the city. Pericles, who, in order to relieve Athens from a number of lazy citizens, whose lives were neither employed in virtuous actions, nor guarded from guilt by habits of industry, planted colonies in Chersonesus, Naxos, Andros, Thrace, and even in Italy, and sent them thither; for this sagacious statesman saw the danger of indulging this growing vice, and wisely took precautions to prevent it. Nothing, indeed, contributes more essentially to the tranquillity of a nation, and to the peaceful demeanor of its inhabitants, than those artificial wants which luxury introduces; for, by creating a demand for the fashionable articles, they engage the attention, and employ the hands of a multitude of manufacturers and artificers, who, if they were left in that restless indolence which the want of work creates, would certainly be unhappy themselves, and in all probability would be fomenting mischief in the minds of others. To suspend only for one week, the vast multitudes that are employed in the several mechanical trades and manufactories in Great Britain, would be to run the risk of involving the metropolis of that great, flourishing, and powerful country, once more in flames; for it would be converting the populace into an aptly disposed train of combustible matter, which being kindled by the least spark of accidental enthusiasm, by the heat of political faction, or, indeed, by their own internal fermentation, would explode into the most flagrant enormities. Nature, it is said, abhors a *vacuum*; and this old peripatetic principle may be properly applied to the intellect, which will embrace any thing, however absurd or criminal, rather than be wholly without an object. The same author also observes, that every man may date the predominance of those desires that disturb his life, and contaminate his conscience, from some unhappy hour when too much leisure exposed him to their incursions; for that *he* has lived with little observation, either on himself or others, who does not know that to be idle is to be vicious. "Many writers of eminence in physic," continues this eminent writer, whose works not only disclose his general acquaintance with life and manners, but a profound knowledge of human nature, "have laid out their diligence upon the consideration of those distempers to which men are exposed by particular states of life; and very learned treatises have been produced upon the maladies of the camp, the sea, and the mines. There are, indeed, few employments which a man accustomed to academical inquiries and medical refinements, would not find reason for declining, as dangerous to health, did not his learning or experience inform him, that almost every occupation, however inconvenient or formidable, is happier and safer than *a life of sloth*. The necessity of action is not only demonstrable from the fabric of the body, but evident from observation of the universal practice of mankind; who for the preservation of health in those whose rank or wealth exempts them from the necessity of lucrative labors, have invented sports and diversions, though not of equal use to the world with manual trades, yet of equal fatigue to those who practice them, and differing only from the drudgery of the husbandman or manufacturer, as they are acts of choice, and therefore performed without the painful sense of compulsion. The huntsman rises early, pursues his game through all the dangers and obstructions of the chase, swims rivers, and scales precipices, till he returns home, no less harassed than the soldier, and has, perhaps, sometimes incurred as great hazard of wounds and death; yet he has no motive to excite his ardor; he is neither subject to the command of a general, nor dreads the penalties of neglect or disobedience: he has neither profits nor honors to expect from his perils and conquests: but acts with the hope of mural or civic garlands, and must content himself with the praise of his tenants and companions. But such is the constitution of man, that *labor is its own reward*; nor will any external incitements be requisite, if it be considered how much happiness is gained, and how much misery escaped, by frequent and violent agitation of the body. Ease is the most that can be hoped from a sedentary and inactive habit; but ease is a mere neutral state, between pain and pleasure. The dance of spirits, the bound of vigor, readiness of enterprise, and defiance of fatigue, are reserved for him that braces his nerves, and hardens his fibres; that keeps his limbs pliant with motion; and, by frequent exposure fortifies his frame against the common accidents of cold and heat. With ease, however, if it could be secured, many would be content; but nothing terrestrial can be kept at a stand. Ease, if it is not rising into pleasure, will be settling into pain; and whatever hopes the dreams of speculation may suggest, of observing the proportion between retirement and labor, and keeping the body in a healthy state by supplies exactly equal to its weight, we know that, in effect, the vital powers, unexcited by motion, grow gradually languid, decay, and die. It is necessary to that perfection of which our present state is capable, that the mind and body should both be kept in action; that neither the faculties of the one nor the other should be suffered to grow lax or torpid for want of use; that neither health can be purchased by voluntary submission to ignorance, nor knowledge cultivated at the expense of that health, which must enable it either to give pleasure to its possessor, or assistance to others. It is too frequently the pride of students, to despise those amusements which give to the rest of mankind strength of limbs and cheerfulness of heart. Solitude and contemplation are, indeed, seldom consistent with such skill in common exercises or sports, as is necessary to make them practised with delight; and no man is willing to do that of which the necessity is not pressing, when he knows that his awkwardness but makes him ridiculous. I have always admired the wisdom of those by whom our female education was instituted, for having contrived that all women, of whatever condition, should be taught some arts of manufacture, by which the vacuities of recluse and domestic leisure may be filled up. These arts are more necessary, as the weakness of their sex, and the general system of life, debar ladies from many enjoyments, which, by diversifying the circumstances of men, preserve them from being cankered by the rust of their own thoughts. I know not how much of the virtue and happiness of the world may be the consequence of this judicious regulation. Perhaps the most powerful fancy might be unable to figure the confusion and slaughter that would be produced by so many piercing eyes and vivid understandings, turned loose upon mankind, with no other business than to sparkle and intrigue, to perplex and destroy. For my own part, whenever chance brings within my observation a knot of misses busy at their needles, I consider myself as in the school of virtue; and though I have no extraordinary skill in plain work, or embroidery, look upon their operations with as much satisfaction as their governess, because I regard them as providing a security against the most dangerous ensnarers of the soul, by enabling them to exclude idleness from their solitary moments, and with idleness, her attendant train of passions, fancies, chimeras, fears, sorrows, and desires. Ovid and Cervantes will inform them that love has no power but on those whom he catches unemployed: and Hector, in the Iliad, when he sees Andromache overwhelmed with tears, sends her for consolation to the loom and the distaff. Certain it is, that wild wishes, and vain imaginations, never take such firm possession of the mind, as when it is found empty and unemployed."

Idleness, indeed, was the spreading root from which all the vices and crimes of the oriental nuns so luxuriantly branched. Few of them had any taste for science, or were enabled by the habits either of reflection, or industry to charm away the tediousness of solitude, or to relieve that weariness which must necessarily accompany their abstracted situation. The talents with which nature had endowed them were uncultivated; the glimmering lights of reason were obscured by a blind and headlong zeal; and their temper soured by the circumstances of their forlorn conditions. Certain it is, that the only means of avoiding unhappiness and misery in solitude, and perhaps in society also, is to keep the mind continually engaged in, or occupied by, some laudable pursuit. The earliest professors of a life of solitude, although they removed themselves far from the haunts of men, among "caverns deep and deserts idle," where nature denied her sons the most common of her blessings, employed themselves in endeavoring to cultivate the rude and barren soil during those intervals in which they were not occupied in the ordinary labors of religion; and even those whose extraordinary sanctity confined them the whole day in their cells, found the necessity of filling up their leisure, by exercising the manual arts for which they were respectively suited. The rules, indeed, which were originally established in most of the convents, ordained that the time and attention of a monk should never be for a moment vacant or unemployed: but this excellent precept was soon rendered obsolete; and the sad consequences which resulted from its non-observance, we have already, in some degree, described.

Chapter VIII
Conclusion

The anxiety with which I have endeavored to describe the advantages and the disadvantages which, under particular circumstances, and in particular situations, are likely to be experienced by those who devote themselves to solitary retirement, may perhaps, occasion me to be viewed by some as its romantic panegyrist, and by others as its uncandid censor. I shall therefore endeavor, in this concluding chapter, to prevent a misconstruction of my opinion, by explicitly declaring the inferences which ought, in fairness, to be drawn from what I have said.

The advocates for a life of uninterrupted society will, in all probability, accuse me of being a morose and gloomy philosopher; an inveterate enemy to social intercourse; who, by recommending a melancholy and sullen seclusion, and interdicting mankind from enjoying the pleasures of life, would sour their tempers, subdue their affections, annihilate the best feelings of the heart, pervert the noble faculty of reason, and thereby once more plunge the world into that dark abyss of barbarism, from which it has been so happily rescued by the establishment and civilization of society.

The advocates for a life of continual solitude will most probably, on the other hand, accuse me of a design to deprive the species of one of the most pleasing and satisfactory delights, by exciting an unjust antipathy, raising an unfounded alarm, depreciating the uses, and aggravating the abuses, of solitude; and by these means endeavoring to encourage that spirit of licentiousness and dissipation which so strongly mark the degeneracy, and tend to promote the vices of the age.

The respective advocates for these opinions, however, equally mistake the intent and view I had in composing this treatise. I do sincerely assure them, that it was very far from my intention to cause a relaxation of the exercise of any of the civil duties of life; to impair in any degree, the social dispositions of the human heart; to lessen any inclination to rational retirement: or to prevent the beneficent practice of *self-communion*, which solitude is best calculated to promote. The fine and generous philanthropy of that mind which, entertaining notions of universal benevolence, seeks to feel a love for, and to promote the good of, the whole human race, can never be injured by an attachment to domestic pleasures, or by cultivating the soft and gentle affections which are only to be found in the small circles of private life, and can never be truly enjoyed, except in the bosom of love, or the arms of friendship: nor will an occasional and rational retirement from the tumults of the world lessen any of the noble sympathies of the human heart: but on the contrary, by enlarging those ideas and feelings which have sprung from the connexions and dependencies which its votary may have formed with individuals, and by generalizing his particular interests and concerns, may enable him to extend the *social principle* and increase the circle of his benevolence.

> God loves from whole to parts; but human soul
>
> Must rise from *individual* to *whole*.
>
> Self love but serves the virtuous mind to wake,
>
> As the small pebble stirs the peaceful lake;
>
> The centre mov'd, a circle straight succeeds;
>
> Another still, and still another spreads;
>
> Friend, parent, neighbor, first it will embrace;
>
> His country next; and next, all human race.

The chief design of this work was, to exhibit the necessity of combining the uses of solitude with those of society; to show, in the strongest light, the advantages they may mutually derive from each other; to convince mankind of the danger of running into either extreme; to teach the advocate for uninterrupted society, how highly all the social virtues may be improved, and its vices easily abandoned, by habits of solitary abstraction; and the advocate for continual solitude, how much that indocility and arrogance of character which is contracted by a total absence from the world, may be corrected by the urbanity of society, and by the company and conversation of the learned and polite.

Petrarch, while in the prime of life, and amidst the happiest exertions of his extraordinary genius, quitted all the seducing charms of society, and retired from love and Avignon, to indulge his mind in literary pursuits, and to relieve his heart, from the unfortunate passion by which it was enthralled. No situation, he conceived, was so favorable for these purposes as the highly romantic and delightful solitude of Vaucluse. It was situated within view of the Mediterranean sea, in a little valley, inclosed by a semicircular barrier of rocks, on a plain as beautiful as the vale of Tempe. The rocks were high, bold, and grotesque; and the valley was divided by a river, along the banks of which were meadows and pastures of a perpetual verdure. A path on the left side of the river, led, by gentle windings, to the head of this vast amphitheatre. At the foot of the highest rock, and directly in front of the valley, was a prodigious cavern, hollowed by the hand of nature, from whence arose a spring almost as celebrated as that of Helicon. The gloom of the cavern, which was accessible when the waters were low, was tremendous. It consisted of two excavations; the one forming an arch of sixty feet high; and the other, which was within, of thirty feet. In the centre of this subterraneous rock was an oval basin, of one hundred and eight feet diameter, into which that copious stream which forms the river Sorgia rises silently, without even a jet or bubble. The depth of this basin has eluded all attempts to fathom it. In this charming retreat, while he vainly endeavored, during a period of twenty years, to forget, he enabled himself to endure the absence of his beloved Laura, and to compare, with the highest satisfaction, the pure pleasures of rural retirement with the false joys of a vicious and corrupted court, the manners and principles of which, indeed, he had always had good sense enough to discover and despise. But this solitude, with all its charms, could not at length prevent him from returning to the more splendid and busy scenes of public life. The advantages he had derived from a retreat of twenty years, would, he conceived, enable him to mix with the world without the danger of being corrupted by its vices; and after reasoning with himself for some time in this way, he suddenly abandoned the peaceful privacy of Vaucluse, and precipitated himself into the gayest and most active scenes of a luxurious city. The inhabitants of Avignon were amazed to behold the hermit of Vaucluse, the tender fugitive from love, the philosophic contemner of society, who could scarcely exist, except in the midst of romantic rocks and flowery forests, shining all at once the bright star of the fashionable hemisphere, and the choice spirit of every private and public entertainment.

> We're sadly ignorant, when we hope to find
>
> In shades a med'cine for a troubled mind;
>
> Wan grief will haunt us wheresoe'er we go,
>
> Sigh in the breeze, and in the streamlet flow:
>
> There pale inaction pines his life away,
>
> And satiate, curses the return of day;
>
> There love, insatiate, rages wild with pain,
>
> Endures the blast, or plunges in the main;
>
> There superstition broods o'er all her fears
>
> And yells of demons in the zephyr hears
>
> He who a hermit is resolv'd to dwell,

And bids a social life a long farewell,

Is impious.

It has already been observed, upon the authority of a very accurate and profound observer of nature, that a very extraordinary temperament of mind and constitution of body are required to sustain, with tranquillity and endurance, the various fatigues of continued solitude; and certain it is, that a human creature who is constantly pent up in seclusion, must, if he be not of a very exalted character, soon become melancholy and miserable. Happiness, like every other valuable quality, cannot be completely possessed, without encountering many dangers, and conquering many difficulties. The prize is great, but the task is arduous. A healthy body, and vigorous mind, are as essentially necessary to the enterprise, as equal courage and fortitude are to its success. The bold adventurer, who, destitute of these resources, quits the bays and harbors of society, shallow, rocky, and dangerous, as they undoubtedly are, and commits himself to the wild and expansive sea of solitude, will sink into its deep and disastrous bed without a hold to save him from destruction. The few instances we have already given, to which many more might easily be added, furnish unequivocal testimony of the truth of this grand precept, *it is not good for man to be alone*: which was given by the great Author of nature, and imprinted in characters sufficiently legible on the human heart.

God never made a solitary man:

'Twould jar the concord of his general plan.

Should man through nature solitary roam,

His will his sovereign, every where his home,

What force would guard him from the lion's jaw?

What swiftness save him from the panther's paw?

Or should fate lead him to some safer shore,

Where panthers never prowl, nor lions roar,

Where liberal nature all her charms bestows,

Suns shine, birds sing, flowers bloom, and water flows,

Still discontented, though such glories shone

He'd sigh and murmur to be there alone.

Content cannot be procured, except by social intercourse, or a judicious communion with those whom congenial tastes, and similar talent and dispositions, point out for our companions. The civilization of man, from whence the species derive such happy consequences, results entirely from a proper management of the *social principles*; even the source of his support, the melioration of the otherwise rude and unprofitable earth, can only be attained by social combination. How erroneous a notion, therefore, must the minds of those men have formed of "their being's end and aim," and how strong must their antipathies to the species be, who like a certain celebrated French hermit, would choose a station among the craters of Vesuvius, as a place which afforded them greater security than the society of mankind! The idea of being able to produce our own happiness from the stores of amusement and delight which we ourselves may possess, independently of all communication with, or assistance from others, is certainly extremely flattering to the natural pride of man; but even if this were possible, and that a solitary enthusiast could work up his feelings to a higher and more lasting degree of felicity, than an active inhabitant of the world, amid all its seducing vices and enchanting follies, is capable of enjoying, it would not follow that society is not the province of all those whom peculiar circumstances have not unfitted for its duties and enjoyments. It is, indeed, a false and deceitful notion, that a purer stream of happiness is to be found in the delightful bowers of solitude than in the busy walks of men. Neither of these stations enjoy exclusively this envied stream: for it flows along the vale of peace, which lies between the two extremes; and those who follow it with a steady pace, without deviating too widely from its brink on either side, will reach its source, and taste it at its spring. But devious, to a certain degree, must be the walk; for the enjoyments of life are best attained by being varied with judgment and discretion. The finest joys grow nauseous to the taste when the cup of pleasure is drained to its dregs. The highest delight loses its attraction by too frequent recurrence. It is only by a proper mixture and combination of the pleasures of society with those of solitude, of the gay and lively recreations of the world with the serene and tranquil satisfactions of retirement, that we can enjoy each in its highest relish. Life is intolerable without society; and society loses half its charms by being too eagerly and constantly pursued. Society, indeed, by bringing men of congenial minds and similar dispositions together, uniting them by a community of pursuits, and a reciprocal sympathy of interests, may greatly assist the cause of truth and virtue, by advancing the means of human knowledge and multiplying the ties of human affections; and so far as the festive board, the lively dance, the brilliant coterie, and other elegant and fashionable pastimes, contribute to these ends, they are truly valuable, and deserve, not only encouragement, but approbation. On this principle, the various clubs which are formed by artizans, and other inferior orders in society, ought to be respected. The mind, in order to preserve its useful activity and proper tone, must be occasionally relaxed, which cannot be so beneficially effected as by means of associations founded on the pursuit of common pleasure. A friendly meeting, or a social entertainment, exhilarates the spirits, exercises the faculties of the mind;

calls forth the feelings of the heart, and creates, when properly formed and indulged, a reciprocity of kindness, confidence, and esteem. It softens the severity of virtue, while it strengthens and enforces its effects. I therefore sincerely exhort my disciples not to absent themselves morosely from public places, nor to avoid the social throng; which cannot fail to afford to judicious, rational, and feeling minds, many subjects both of amusement and instruction. It is true, that we cannot relish the pleasures, and taste the advantages of society, without being able to give a patient hearing to the tongue of folly, to excuse error, to bear with infirmity, to view mediocrity of talents without scorn, and illiberality of sentiment without retort; to indulge frivolity of behavior, and even to forgive rudeness of manners: but the performance of these conditions meets with its own reward; for it is scarcely credible, how very much our own tempers and dispositions are meliorated, and our understandings improved, by bearing with the different tempers, and humoring the perverse dispositions of others; we experience by such a conduct the high delight of pleasing others, and the great advantage of improving ourselves.

Delightful, however, as social pleasures naturally are to the human mind; necessary as they certainly are, under proper regulations, to the preservation of the spirits; and beneficial as they may undoubtedly be rendered, by judicious choice and wise reflection, it is not every person who withdraws himself from the highly colored scenes of public life, to the shades of privacy and retirement, that deserves the imputation generally cast on such characters, of being inclined to sullenness and misanthropy. There are many who seek the retreats of solitude, for the very purpose of rendering their efforts more useful to society; many who relinquish the endearments of private friendship, and the applauses of public approbation, only the more nobly to deserve them; and many, whose souls are so bitterly tormented by the anguish of misfortune, and the sickness of sorrow, that they find no relief from society, and recede from its scenes to avoid giving disturbance to that gayety which they are incapable of enjoying, and to prevent their fractious feelings from molesting any but themselves. There are others who retire from the world to pursue objects the most glorious to the individual, and most useful to mankind; the attainment of which can only be hoped for from the advantages which solitude affords. Glowing with a sublime and generous spirit, they sacrifice the joys of life, the charms of society, and even the advantages of health, to show their attachment to the species; and, immured from the sight of this world, toil, with indefatigable industry, for its benefit, without expecting any other reward than the satisfaction resulting from the sense of having promoted the interest, and advanced the happiness of their fellow creatures. So also,

Sage reflection, bent with years;

Conscious virtue, void of fears;

Muffled silence, wood-nymph shy;

Meditation's piercing eye;

Halcyon peace on moss reclin'd;

Retrospect, that sears the mind;

Rapt, earth-gazing reverie;

Blushing, artless modesty;

Health, that snuffs the morning air;

Full-ey'd truth, with bosom bare;

Inspiration, nature's child,

Seek the solitary wild.

The state of the mind, if properly consulted, will discover whether solitude may be safely indulged. The bosom that, amidst the gay delights and luxurious pleasures of the world, feels a rising discontent and uneasiness, may try the retreats of solitude without danger: and if, after a certain period, an attachment to its mild and tranquil scenes continues, and the heart enjoys that quietude and content which it before so vainly wished to experience, society may be advantageously relinquished. The patient may, under such circumstances, safely indulge the natural inclinations of the mind, and gratify the habitual feelings of his heart: he may then exclaim in the language of the poet,

"Oh! snatch me swift from those tumultuous scenes,

To lonely groves and sweetly verdant greens,

To where religion, peace, and comfort dwell,

And cheer with heavenly rays the lonely cell:

To where no ruffling winds, no raging seas,

Disturb the mind amidst its pensive ease:

Each passion calm; where mild affections shine,

The soul-enjoying quietude divine:

Unknown in private or in public strife,

Soft sailing down the placid stream of life:

Aw'd by no terrors, by no cares perplex'd;

My life a gentle passage to the next."

But when that delightful tranquillity of mind, which an excess of social pleasure has impaired or destroyed, is not restored to its original purity by the uninterrupted quietude of seclusion, it may fairly be concluded, that there is some natural and constitutional defect, that defeats the remedy, and prevents the soul from tasting that serenity which is so essential to the enjoyment of human happiness. Under such circumstances it is dangerous to indulge the pleasures of solitude; the sufferer should fly back to society; cultivate the duties of active life, and solicit, with temperate indulgence, its more agreeable enjoyments. For, although the pleasures and occupations of the world cannot eradicate this species of intellectual disease, they may, by being judiciously followed, suspend its progress, and alleviate its pangs. That case must always be desperate, when the antidote is too weak to reach the poison, or to counteract its operation. A pious resignation to his fate can alone afford relief.

> "Oh! as it pleases thee, thou Power Supreme,
>
> To drive my bark thro' life's more rapid stream,
>
> If lowering storms my destin'd course attend,
>
> And ocean rage 'til this black voyage shall end,
>
> Let ocean rage, and storms indignant roar,
>
> I bow submissive and resign'd adore:
>
> Resign'd adore, in various changes tri'd;
>
> Thy own lov'd Son my anchor and my guide:
>
> Resign'd adore, whate'er thy will decree;
>
> My faith in Jesus, and my hope in Thee;
>
> And humbly wait 'til, through a sea of woes,
>
> I reach the wish'd-for harbor of repose."

There are, however, circumstances under which it is absolutely necessary to retire from the world, in order to avoid the recurrence of sentiments and feelings that are pregnant with unhappiness. To a mind that feels unconquerable disgust of the manners and maxims of a world which it cannot reform; to a heart that turns with horror from the various sights the world exhibits of human wo, which he is incapable of relieving; to a bosom that is stung by the various vices which he cannot prevent or restrain, and which are hourly practised among the sons of men, retirement becomes an obligation which the justice that every good man owes to his own felicity demands. The impulse of solitude may in such cases be conscientiously indulged, in the firmest confidence of its rectitude. It is a retreat necessary to the preservation, not only of happiness but of virtue;

and the world itself may be benefited by its effects. Removed from the sad scenes of inactivity, wretchedness, and guilt, the tender feelings of pity are regulated with composure; the mind views its own operations with nicer discrimination; the high sense of virtue is rendered less indignant; and the hatred against vice more temperate and discerning. The violent emotions which created the disgusting pain gently subside; and as our reflections on the condition of human nature prevail, the soul feels how incumbent it is to endeavor to bear with the follies, to alleviate the miseries, and to reform the vices of mankind; while the leisure and quietude which solitude affords, enables a man, who has thus retired, to point out the most likely means of accomplishing the ends which his lonely meditation, and philanthropic feelings, have generally inspired.

> "With aspect mild, and elevated eye,
>
> Behold him seated on a mount serene,
>
> Above the fogs of sense, and passion's storm.
>
> All the black cares and tumults of this life,
>
> Like harmless thunder breaking at his feet,
>
> Excite his pity, nor impair his peace.
>
> Earth's genuine sons, the sceptred and the slave,
>
> A mingled mob! a wandering herd! he sees,
>
> Bewilder'd in the vale; in all unlike,
>
> His full reverse in all! What higher praise
>
> What stronger demonstration of the right?
>
> Himself too much he prizes to be proud,
>
> And nothing thinks so great in man as man.
>
> Too dear he holds man's interest to neglect
>
> Another's welfare, or his right invade.
>
> Wrong he sustains with temper, looks on heav'n,
>
> Nor stoops to think his injurer his foe;
>
> But looks with gentle pity round, to find
>
> How he can best relieve another's wo,
>
> Or hush the vicious passions into peace."

Those who have passed their lives in the domestic privacies of retirement; who have been only used to the soft and gentle offices of friendship, and to the tender endearments of love; who have formed their notion of virtue from those bright images which the purity of religion, the perfection of moral sentiments, and the feelings of an affectionate heart, have planted in their minds, are too apt to yield to the abhorrence and disgust they must unavoidably feel on a first view of the artificial manners and unblushing vices of the world. Issuing from the calm retreats of simplicity and innocence, and fondly hoping to meet with more enlarged perfection in the world, their amiable, just and benevolent dispositions are shocked at the sour severities, the sordid selfishness, the gross injustice, the base artifices, and the inhuman cruelties, which deform the fairest features of social life, and disgrace the best famed fabric of human polity. Revolting, however, as this disappointment must certainly be, and grievously as the feelings of such characters be wounded on their entering the world, it is a cowardly desertion of their duty to shrink from the task, and withdraw their services from their fellow creatures. Constituted as society is, human happiness, and the improvement of the species, materially depend upon the active concurrence of every individual in the general scheme of nature; and the man who withholds his assistance to promote the public good, loosens or destroys a link in that chain of things, by which the whole is intended to be kept together and preserved. The doctrine, therefore cannot be too forcibly inculcated, that is indispensably incumbent on every individual so to accommodate himself to the manners of his contemporaries, and the temper of the times, that he may have an opportunity of promoting the happiness of others, while he increases, his own; of extending the scale of human knowledge by his social industry; of relieving distress by his bounty; and of exhibiting the deformities of vice, and the beauties of virtue, both by his precept and example. And this sacred obligation, by which every good man feels himself so firmly bound to promote the welfare and happiness of his fellow creatures, of course enjoins him to shun, with equal perseverance, the giddy multitude in their pursuits of lawless pleasure, and to avoid the thoughtless votaries, and baneful orgies, of wit, intemperance, and sensual debauchery. This is best effected by every individual forming a rational scheme of domestic enjoyment, and engaging in some useful occupation, in which neither the frivolous pursuits of the vainly busy, the ostentatious parade of the richly proud, the faithless pleasures of the unthinking gay, the insatiable anxieties of avarice, nor the distracting compunctions of vice, shall form any part; but in which, with a few amiable and faithful friends, he shall pass the intervals of virtuous industry, or charitable exertion, in the bosom of a fond and cheerful family, whose mutual endearments and affections will confer on each other the highest happiness human nature is capable of enjoying.

> Active in indolence, abroad who roam
>
> In quest of happiness, which dwells at home,

With vain pursuits fatigued, at length will find

Its real dwelling is a virtuous mind.

Retirement, however, when it is not inconsistent with our duties to society, or injurious to those family interests which it is one of our principal foundations of happiness to promote, is capable of producing the most beneficial effects on our minds. The self-communion which must accompany a wise and rational solitude, not only fosters and confirms our virtuous inclinations, but detects and expels those latent vices which have secretly crept into and corrupted the heart. It induces a habit of contemplation, which invigorates the faculties of the soul; raises them to the highest energies, and directs them to purposes more elevated and noble than it was possible for them, amidst the business and pleasures of public life, to attain. It tends, indeed, to unfold the powers of the mind to so great an extent, that we are ashamed of having thought that our talents were confined within the limits we had prescribed, and blush at the ignorance and cowardice by which we were deceived. The activity of genius is unlimited, and the measure of its effects depends entirely upon a steady exertion of its powers. A courageous and persevering industry is capable of surmounting every difficulty, and of performing the highest achievements. A sense of intellectual weakness so far from being indulged, ought to be combated with fortitude and resolution, until it is completely destroyed. The human mind, like a noble tree, extends its branches widely round, and raises them to the skies, in proportion as the soil on which it grows is more or less cultivated and manured: but not being fixed to any certain spot, its growth may be improved to any size, by transplanting it to the soil in which it most delights to dwell. By that firm reliance on its natural strength, that indefatigable exertion of its improved powers, that steady observance of its successful operations, that warm and active zeal for excellence to which it is invited by the advantages, and encouraged by the opportunities, which seclusion affords, it will ascend from one stage of improvement to another, from acquisition to acquisition; and, by a gradual and steady progress, reach a comprehensive elevation, as great and surprising as it was once thought visionary and unattainable. To these sublime and noble effects of human intellect, solitude is the sincerest guide and most powerful auxiliary; and he who aspires to mental and moral excellence, whose soul is anxious to become both great and good, will, of course, seek its inspiring shades.

Solitude, indeed, under any circumstances, can only become injurious by being carried to excess, or by being misapplied; and what is there that will not, by being abused, or misapplied, be rendered equally injurious? The highest advantages society is capable of conferring, the loftiest flights of fancy, the best affections of the heart, the greatest strength of body, the happiest activity of the mind, the elements of fire and water, the blessings of liberty, and, in short, all the excellent gifts of Providence, as well as all the ingenious contrivances of man, may, by these means be perverted, their uses destroyed, their ends and objects defeated, and their operations and effects rendered extensively mischievous and detrimental.

The general disadvantages which solitude is certainly capable of producing, cannot be lessened by conceding to its adversaries, that it is, when sought under unfavorable circumstances, inauspicious to human happiness. It would be overstepping the sacred boundaries of truth, and violating the rights of candor, not to admit that irrational solitude frequently overclouds the reason, contracts the understanding, vitiates the manners, inflames the passions, corrupts the imagination, sours the temper, and debases the whole character of its votaries. Nor is it necessary to deny, that many of them instead of employing the delightful leisure which retirement affords, to hush the jarring passions, to chastise the fancy, to elevate and adorn the mind, and to reform and meliorate the heart, have been too often occupied in the most frivolous pursuits, and in the indulgence of the most sordid and criminal desires.

But these instances in which the pure and peaceful retreats of solitude have been tainted and disturbed by the vicious and turbulent desires of the world, only demonstrate the infirm, corrupt, and imperfect nature of the species, and not in the smallest degree, depreciate the value of those high advantages which result from occasional and well regulated solitude.

It is said, by a celebrated German writer, in a poetical personification of solitude, that she holds in one hand a cup of bliss, in which she presents unceasing sweets to the lips of the happy; and in the other grasps an envenomed dagger, which she plants with increasing tortures in the bosom of the wretched; but this must be considered as the language of the muse, and mere flight of poetic fancy; except, indeed, so far as it tends to enforce the idea, that virtue will always be happy, and vice forever miserable; for retirement, while it pours the balm of comfort into the aching bosom of the unfortunate, and offers a cordial, cheering as nectar, to the drooping spirits of the wise and virtuous, only operates as a corrosive, agonizing poison, on the constitutions of the weak and vicious.

It is a gross mistake, to suppose that the pleasures of social life are incompatible with the benefits to be derived from solitude. They may not only be intermingled with, but made mutually to aid and augment each other. Solitude may surely be enjoyed without undergoing an exile from the world; and society may be freely mixed with, without absolutely renouncing the pleasures of retirement. The circumstances of life, indeed, call loudly on every mind to interchange the pursuits of activity and scenes of quietude and repose. The alliance of solitude and society is necessary to the perfection not only of the intellectual character, but to the corporeal constitution of man. To conclude that the duties of life must necessarily be neglected by devoting a portion of our time to solitude, is much more erroneous than to conclude that those duties are not always fulfilled amidst the pleasures or business of society.

Daily observation proves most clearly, that many of the charms, and some of the benefits, of rural retreat, may be enjoyed without retiring to any very considerable distance from the metropolis, the seat of social joys and interested activity. Petrarch, during his residence in the city of Parma, though extremely flattered by the friendship shown him, was glad to steal from public life as often as he could, and to indulge the high delight he naturally felt in wandering through the fields and woods which surrounded the metropolis. One day, led by his love of exercise, he passed the river of Lenza, which is three miles from Parma, and found himself in the territory of Rhegio, in a forest which is called Sylva Plana, or Low Wood: though it is situated upon a hill, from whence are discovered the Alps, and all Cisalpine Gaul. Aged oaks, whose heads seemed to touch the clouds, sheltered the avenues of the forest from the rays of the sun: while the fresh breezes which descended from the neighboring mountains, and the little rivulets which brawled along its skirts, tempered the meridian heats of the day, and preserved to the earth, even in the greatest droughts, a soft verdure, enamelled with the finest flowers. Birds of every kind warbled forth their rural songs from the thick coverts, while deer, and every animal of the chase, sported through the purlieus. In the middle of this beautiful forest nature had formed a romantic theatre, which, from its enchanting decorations, she seemed to have designed for the residence of the muses. The charms of this delightful retreat struck the mind of Petrarch with a sort of inspiration, and revived so strongly his original taste for solitude that on his return to Parma, he endeavored to procure some spot near the environs of the city, to which he might occasionally retire from the fatigues of his archdeaconry, and indulge his mind in the blessings of innocence, and the delights of rural repose. The industry of his inquiries soon furnished him with a small cottage, exactly suited to his wishes, situated at the end of the city, near the abbey of St. Anthony. To this place he fondly and frequently retired, whenever he could escape from the duties of his church, and the invitations of his friends. The superiority of his talents had at this time attracted the attention and applause of mankind; and his engaging manners secured to him the respect and esteem of the nobles of Parma, who besieged him with the most friendly and flattering importunities to partake of their daily parties of pleasure. Petrarch, however, had formed notions of happiness very foreign to those which result from the society of luxurious lords or fashionable females, to whom, in general poetry afforded no delight, nor philosophy instruction; and the companions to whom he could afford neither amusement nor information, were not likely to afford him much satisfaction. The quiet and simple pleasures of retirement were more delightful to his mind than all the elegances and splendors of Parma; but this partiality to retirement did not induce him to renounce the rational society which a few select friends, with whom he had closely connected himself, was occasionally capable of affording him. "So conveniently," says he, "is this delightful cottage situated, that I enjoy all the advantages of rural retirement, and yet retain within my reach all the pleasures with which this gay and elegant city abounds. The society of a few select friends recreates my mind whenever it is distracted by the anxieties of study, or stagnated by the stilness of solitude; and when I am satiated with the pleasures of the town, I fly with rapture to the sweet repose, and to all the interesting and endearing occupations of this charming retreat. Oh! may the kindness of fortune long indulge me in the enjoyment of this neutral state; this happy alternation of rural tranquillity and convivial solace! a state of felicity to which neither the anchorites of Egypt, nor the philosophers of Greece, ever attained. In this humble abode, let me quietly pass the remainder of my days, unseduced by the charms of greatness, and uninterrupted by the pleasures of the world. Fly, all ye vain delusions and fantastic dreams, from this cottage of content, and seek your native territories, the palaces of princes, and the altars of ambition!" The voice of wisdom and virtue calls aloud on every man to adopt the scheme of happiness which Petrarch so successfully practised. By thus dividing our time between the busy cares and innocent amusements of public life, and the studious and tranquil pleasures of retirement, between the gay pursuits of personal gratifications, and the more noble and elevated exercises of intellect, we may avoid the dangers of contracting, on the one hand, a passion for light and frivolous dissipation, and on the other a joyless disposition to misanthropic severity; and may shun the most, if not all the evil consequences which either solitude or society is capable of producing, which when indulged irrationally, or indiscreetly, in general prove the Scylla or Charybdis of our lives.

These are the observations which it has occurred to me to make upon the advantages or disadvantages with which those important means of human happiness are respectively pregnant. I can truly say, that I have felt, whenever the cares of life, and the duties of my profession, have allowed me leisure to retire, the most sublime and satisfactory enjoyment from solitude; and I sincerely wish that every one who is disposed to taste it, may receive the same comfort and pleasure from its charms. But I exhort them, while they enjoy the sacred blessings of repose, not to neglect the social virtues, the consolations of friendship, or the endearments of love; but so manage the wants of nature, and arrange the business and concerns of life, as to find an adequate portion of leisure for the noble duties of retirement, as well as for company and conversation of the world. May they in short, enjoy the admiration and esteem of their friends, and a complacent approbation of their own conduct, without losing that relish for the pleasures of rational retirement, by which alone these high advantages are most likely to be gained.

To love all mankind, and to promote, to the utmost of our power, the happiness of all those with whom we are more intimately connected, is the highest injunction both of morality and religion. But this important duty certainly does not require that we should surrender ourselves with servile obedience, or abject submission, to any one, however superior he may be, either in talents, in station, or in merit. On the contrary, it is the duty of every one, not only to cultivate the inclination, but to reserve the power of retiring occasionally from the world, without indulging a disposition to renounce its society or contemn its manners.

While we assert, with manly resolution, the independent spirit of human nature, our happiness may be considerably augmented, by extracting from the multitudinous affairs of the world, the various enjoyments and wise instructions it is capable of affording. Society is the school of wisdom, and solitude the temple of virtue. In the one we learn the art of living with comfort among our fellow creatures, and in the other, of living with quietude by ourselves. A total retreat from the world would place us aside from that part which Providence chiefly intended us to act; but without occasional retreat it is certain that we must act that part very ill. There will be neither consistency in the conduct, nor dignity in the character, of one who sets apart no share of his time for meditation and reflection. "In the heat and bustle of life," says an eloquent preacher, "while passion is every moment throwing false colors on the objects around us, nothing can be viewed in a just light. If you wish that reason should exert her native power, you must step aside from the crowd into the cold and silent shade. It is thus that with sober and steady eye she examines what is good or ill, what is wise or foolish, in human conduct: she looks back on the past; she looks forward to a future: and forms plans not for the present moment only, but for the whole life. How should that man discharge any part of his duty aright, who never suffers his passions to cool? And how should his passions cool, who is engaged, without interruption, in the tumults of the world? This incessant stir may be called the *perpetual drunkenness of life*. It raises that eager fermentation of spirit, which will be ever sending forth the dangerous fumes of rashness and folly. Whereas he who mingles rational retreat with worldly affairs, remains calm and master of himself. He is not whirled round, and rendered giddy by the agitation of the world: but from that sacred retirement, in which he has been conversant among higher objects, comes forth into the world with manly tranquillity, fortified by principles which he has formed, and prepared for whatever may befal."

Sweet solitude! when life's gay hours are past,

Howe'er we range, in thee we fix at last.

Tossed through tempestuous seas, the voyage o'er,

Pale we look back and bless the friendly shore.

Our own strict judges, our past life we scan

And ask if glory hath enlarged the span;

If bright the prospect we the grave defy,

Trust future ages, and contented die.

www.ingramcontent.com/pod-product-compliance
Lightning Source LLC
Chambersburg PA
CBHW051454130726
47987CB00005B/2308